WE USE WHAT WE HAVE

RECIPES

WE USE WHAT WE HAVE

101 EASY WEEKNIGHT MEALS

RECIPES

ALEX MacLAREN

Countryman Press

An Imprint of W. W. Norton & Company
Independent Publishers Since 1923

Printed in China
First Edition

For information about special discounts for bulk purchases, please contact W. W. Norton Special Sales at specialsales@wwnorton.com or 800-233-4830

Manufacturing by TOPPAN Leefung
Book design by Allison Chi
Production manager: Devon Zahn

Countryman Press
www.countrymanpress.com

An imprint of W. W. Norton & Company, Inc.
500 Fifth Avenue, New York, NY 10110
www.wwnorton.com

Authorized EU representative: EAS, Mustamäe tee 50, 10621 Tallinn, Estonia

ISBN 978-1-324-11185-6

1 2 3 4 5 6 7 8 9 0

To all the home cooks who'd rather spend their money on other things . . . We use what we have.

CONTENTS

INTRODUCTION

HOW I LEARNED TO COOK . . .

You'd think with my wing-it-in-the-kitchen attitude, I'd have grown up in the kitchen watching my mom, but you'd be wrong. As the daughter of a corporate mama who viewed making supper as another chore on her to-do list, almost none of my cooking skills were passed down from family—in fact there was a running joke that my mom couldn't boil water when she and my dad got married. So how did I go from being a boxed macaroni and frozen pizza kid to teaching over a million people how to play real-life *Chopped* at home?

I will give credit where due: My mom did learn a handful of recipes . . . and made them on rotation for about eleven years. Then in the fifth grade I befriended Sophie. Sophie was the middle child of three with a close-knit extended family. To me, an extroverted only child, Sophie's weekly family meals were what dreams are made of. Kids were expected to pitch in, and you always wanted to cook because the other task was dishes. We were given a meal and loose instructions but never recipes. Being entrusted with feeding a crowd and actually making food people wanted to eat was amazing. (It's proof that kids do want to contribute, and they are way more capable than we sometimes give them credit or opportunity for.)

Well, cooking a couple times per month wasn't enough for me, so I started cooking at home too. And my mother was *thrilled*. In the beginning there were lots of packaged foods, but as my confidence in the kitchen grew, I started reading cookbooks, meal planning, and eventually grocery shopping. Now here's where the magic really happened: My mom may not have been a chef, but she had a long career in banking and her teaching me how to shop smart laid the groundwork for the budget-friendly cooking style I have today.

Feeding people is kinda (not just kinda) my thing, and I fully attribute that to the five-star reviews I got on probably mediocre at best meals, which serves as a reminder that if you're just starting your We Use What We Have cooking journey, everyone starts at the beginning, and practice makes progress. Eventually I moved out for university (fun fact: I have both a fine art and an engineering degree), and with the help of the Food Network and Allrecipes.com, I kept cooking for roommates, friends . . . basically whoever was hungry.

While in university, I also got a part-time job as a grocery store cashier. Being a little math-minded and a lot creative, I watched people's buying patterns over the course of four years. What ingredients are always cheap, which sales come up regularly, and what not to buy when you're on a budget. I asked customers about ingredients I wasn't familiar with and how to use them. You may be thinking, "Alex—two degrees and you're not using either of them?" But you really never know where your path will take you, and I'd argue that the skills I learned are a huge component in the successes I've had as a food content creator.

But how did I learn to substitute so well? I basically had a crash course when I had a kid with a food allergy and made the whole family vegan for about two years. My firstborn used to have a dairy intolerance, so I suddenly had to learn to cook and shop completely dairy-free. I went from swapping in nondairy alternatives to making my own from scratch. Then 2020 happened and food felt like the only thing I could control, so control it I did. But nobody else wanted to be vegan, so I learned to make our regular meals, but without the animal products. Eventually I came back around and the kid outgrew the allergy, so you're gonna see a lot of cheese in this book because I *really* missed it!

Cut to having three babies and three reduced-income maternity leaves over five years (in Canada, we can collect unemployment insurance but are typically not paid by our employer while on leave). Luckily, I was no stranger to being on a budget because by the time my youngest came along, so did inflation. Then the company I was working for announced they would be selling—so I took it as a sign to record and share the way I was feeding my family with whoever wanted to listen . . . and that's how the We Use What We Have community was born.

WHAT'S FOR SUPPER TONIGHT? (AND HOW TO USE THIS BOOK)

I love looking through a cookbook for meal plan inspiration, but the reality is, most of the time I'm rummaging through my kitchen trying to figure out what I can make with what I have on hand. And if you're on a budget, that's probably how you should be approaching it too (more on that on page 20).

My goal is for this cookbook to become your go-to guide for figuring out what's for supper tonight and ultimately help you develop your own kitchen management style to make feeding yourself and your family easier. I designed its contents to meet you where you are now, whether you are on a budget, short on time, or new to cooking. And that's exactly why I laid it out the same way my brain works. I've included two ways to search for recipes:

1. By meal type—because if you're like me you're just out here living on vibes and what sounds good *today*, not last week when I planned it. This is 100 percent the reason I've never been able to stick to meal planning. Every time I try it, I end up having to either eat what I'm no longer in the mood for or figure out something else that I *am* in the mood for with the groceries I bought. Almost all my recipes are flexible and include ideas for substitutions, so if you have a bit of groceries you should be able to find something in each section you can successfully throw together.

2. At the core of every meal is probably the protein you thawed (or forgot to). I wanted to make the recipes in this book searchable by protein, so if you have chicken legs, for example, look under bone-in chicken in the index and see what recipe looks good.

My personal goal is always to work myself out of a job, so I have included lots of tips and explanations in each recipe to help you understand my decision-making process. I've also included "Use what you have" substitution tables and alternative cooking-without-a-recipe skills. Food is nourishment, but it's also love and joy, and there's nothing quite like the high of getting rave reviews when you share a meal you made from scratch. I hope your copy of this book becomes a well-used resource and you write your own notes in the margins.

PROTEIN AS THE STAR

At the core of every meal is the main protein—that's just how my brain works and it's probably how yours does too. When I'm grocery shopping, I'm checking the grocery flyer for the best deals on meat. When I'm planning my week, it's straight to the freezer to take my little meat inventory.

All of the recipes in this book use generally more affordable cuts of meat, but the reality is that if you want to keep your grocery bill lower, you still need to shop smart (for more on how to save money on groceries, see page 20). If it's not on sale, I'm going to have to pay more, so I'm probably not buying it. When there's a really good sale I get an extra or two to freeze for later—this makes up my budget-friendly "use what I have" stash.

I know what you're thinking: Won't it get freezer burn? Sales tend to come back up every couple of months, so your goal shouldn't be doomsday prep (and if it is, maybe buy a vacuum sealer)—I'm talking about a little extra so I'm not at the mercy of the two cuts in my store's weekly flyer.

My inventory is in constant rotation, which means I eat things *before* they get freezer burn. I've found this strategy provides me the variety I crave but at a cost my wallet can handle.

MIX IT UP

Just because a recipe calls for a certain cut of meat doesn't mean that's what you have to use. Bone-in chicken cuts are pretty interchangeable, but note that cook time will vary. Pork and beef are both considered red meat and are reasonably interchangeable. If you're making anything stir-fry adjacent, extra-firm tofu works great. Freeze and thaw your tofu ahead if you can, which creates ice pockets. This will not only make it easier to get more water out but also gives the tofu a meatier texture. When it comes to the recipes in this book, I've done the heavy lifting for you by offering protein swaps in nearly all the recipes. For example, if you have chicken drumsticks, there are five recipes that call for bone-in chicken, plus others that you could try using them in.

And believe it or not, you're perfectly capable of learning some basic butchering skills. Sharpen your knife (a sharp knife is a safe knife), look up a quick video, and break down that whole chicken, slice that pork loin into chops, or cube that roast into stew meat.

Another budget tip: Check discount racks and apps, which are for quick sales of food nearing its sell-by date (as a bonus, it also keeps food out of landfills). Freeze these or cook immediately—time is money, friend. If you've been wanting to try but the thought of near-date meat gives you the ick, here's my advice: Employees are trained on inspecting products before listing them, but you need to use your judgment. If it smells funky or is discolored or slimy—toss it and request a refund. It's never worth getting sick over a couple dollars.

The table on page 16 lists cuts that tend to either be lower cost or regularly go on sale, and ultimately most of what you'll find in my recipes.

When I say eggs, does your mind immediately go to breakfast . . . for dinner (or anytime)? They are actually incredibly versatile—from noodles and rice to potato skillets to sandwiches, there are countless ways for eggs to pump a little more protein into your meal. Bonus: Eggs are super quick to make and also super kid friendly.

	MOST AFFORDABLE CUTS
POULTRY	Bone-in chicken, especially thighs, drumsticks, and whole legs Whole turkeys, after holidays Ground turkey, in tubes Frozen breaded chicken (nuggets, etc.)
PORK	Pork chops Pork tenderloin Side ribs Sausages, fresh and smoked Whole hams, after holidays
BEEF	Ground beef, on sale or in tubes Roasts, especially tougher cuts or on sale Stewing beef
SEAFOOD	Salmon trimmings Seafood mix (trimmings; sometimes called chowder mix) Frozen shrimp Frozen white fish (compare weight, as package weight can vary by type of fish)
TOFU	All, but compare prices across brands Extra-firm texture is generally best for most recipes

FORGOT TO THAW SOMETHING? ENTER BEANS, LENTILS, TUNA & NUTS

Look, we've all been there. You get home at the end of the day and realize you forgot to thaw meat for dinner. Or worse, you had that "oh sh*t" moment while you were out and it's been living rent-free in your head ever since. Days like these are exactly why I keep some canned protein options like beans, lentils, tuna, and nuts in my pantry. "But Alex, my family won't eat beans." Listen, I get it, mine also took some time to buy in, and there are still days when they just tolerate them, but I guess that's just the way the bean crumbles. Here are some tips to convert bean haters to bean lovers:

1. **RINSE AND DRAIN** your canned beans and lentils in a colander under water. The number of cooking videos I've seen where people dump the beans into the pot (drained or not) tells me that many of you are not washing off the canned taste. Do you not like beans? Or maybe you just do not like the taste of canned bean water (which between you and me kinda tastes like farts). Rinsing your beans and lentils also reduces the amount of gas those beans will cause you. The exception here is chickpeas: Drain that beautiful canning liquid (known as aquafaba) into another container because you can whip it up and use it as an egg replacement. But still rinse the beans, I beg you.

2. **SEASON, SEASON, SEASON!** Beans and lentils don't taste like much, so if you don't like the taste, you're probably underseasoning. They should for the most part take on the flavor of the dish. I also like to use bouillon to add some of that meat-like flavor back in. And if your beans and lentils still aren't getting the memo, you might be adding the seasoning too late in the cooking process. Season early, season heavily, and simmer long enough to let those flavors meld.

3. **LESS IS MORE . . .** at least when you're starting out. Mixing beans and lentils in with your meat is a great way to stretch your meal without losing that rich flavor you get from meat. They are high in fiber, low in fat, and a great source of protein. The ratio I find works best is approximately 1 cup beans or lentils for every 1 pound (454 g) ground meat. Try this trick next time you make tacos and let me know what you think.

4. **TEXTURE MATTERS.** If I had a dollar for every time I heard "It's not the taste—I can't get past the texture"! I'm gonna hold your hand while I say this: You'll get over it. Now if you have the budget to never eat beans and you really don't want to, this one isn't for you. But beans and lentils are easy, shelf-stable, affordable sources of protein and fiber. They are a staple in many countries' diets because people eat what they can access and afford. Neither myself nor my husband grew up eating beans, so I know firsthand that the more you eat them, the more you'll enjoy them. Which brings me to . . .

5. **CHOOSE WISELY.** Not all beans and lentils are created equal. Some are in my opinion more palatable—gateway beans, if you will. For example, split red lentils basically melt into the dish, while green lentils are bigger, with a thicker outer layer. If your goal, like mine, is to make beans and lentils somewhat ignorable in the meal, then here are some of our favorites, as well as other pantry proteins we keep on hand (see more details on page 23):

   - White kidney beans (cannellini)
   - Split red lentils
   - Black beans
   - Brown lentils
   - Homestyle baked beans
   - Chickpeas
   - Canned tuna
   - Canned chicken
   - Peanut butter
   - Cashews

And if you're still feeling anti-beans, there's always canned tuna, nuts, and nut butters. Tuna isn't just for sandwiches anymore. Try it in pasta or rice—and remember to drain the can (unless you love tuna water, then carry on!). Or throw a couple handfuls of cashews into a stir-fry or mix peanut butter into the sauce.

BUT WHERE'S THE PROTEIN?!

Every time I skip meat or use just a small portion of meat in a video, I get comments like "Where's the protein?" or "Not enough protein!" or "My husband would never eat this." First of all, *my* husband doesn't complain when I cook, and if he doesn't like what I've made, he's a grown adult with free will of his own; he's perfectly capable of shopping and cooking for himself.

Second, we've been conditioned to believe that you need meat in every meal, which just isn't true. For most healthy people, nutrition matters more across a whole day or a few days than at each individual meal. So, before you swear off meatless Mondays, know that when you eat a variety of whole foods, you should be getting enough protein without having to overthink it. But if you're concerned, please consult your doctor.

Simply put, adding beans or lentils is an easy way to stretch meat without losing flavor and texture. Here are some pairings I like:

MEAT	WITH
Ground beef	Black beans, red kidney beans, brown lentils
Chicken, shrimp	Chickpeas
Ground poultry	White kidney beans (cannellini)
Pork	Baked beans, navy beans

And if you're looking for more ways to cut for your food costs, keep reading . . .

HOW TO SAVE MONEY ON GROCERIES

Groceries have gotten dang expensive, and the reality is, prices will continue to rise year over year. But *don't panic*! Keeping your food costs manageable (without feeling deprived) boils down to three main concepts: reducing waste, shopping smarter, and really learning to cook. So here are my best tips for each of those, and none of them involve spending hours clipping coupons or running to five different stores every week.

Before we get into it, let's clear the air: I don't do all of these things all of the time, and you probably won't either. We also use what we have in terms of time and energy, and saving money does take a little extra effort. I like to think of convenience as a service, and doing things yourself will almost always be cheaper because *you* are performing the service of researching, planning, prepping, and cooking.

Some weeks I'm burning the candle at both ends and I'll pay a little more to cut out some steps. And while I certainly never *want* to spend the most, sometimes my ultimate goal isn't to spend the least amount possible . . . more on that soon.

REDUCE FOOD WASTE

The harsh truth is that throwing away food you let spoil is equivalent to throwing away money. Now let me be loud and clear: I'm not saying you should eat rotten food (please don't). I'm saying, with a little planning you can prevent this.

- Take a quick grocery inventory every few days and try to use up anything that will spoil soon (try my flowchart on page 41 for some super flexible fridge clean-out recipes to make tonight). Can't look at

another plate of that shepherd's pie you made two days ago? Perfect freezer meal for that extra-long day you have next week. Absence makes the heart (and stomach) grow fonder.

- Stop buying greens if they always rot in your fridge (or get baby spinach instead—you can freeze that!). If you can't think of how you'll use something up, maybe don't buy it in the first place. That $3 bag of avocados is a moot point if you'll only eat one (this last one is for me). This goes for everything, BTW, not just produce: It's not cheaper if you throw it out.
- On that note: Cook smaller portions. If you love leftovers, this one isn't for you, but unfortunately my family has a cook-once/eat-once mentality. And as much as it sucks, that's probably not going to change. You know when people adopt a big dog that needs all the walking thinking they'll suddenly become outdoorsy or fit? Cut to a year later and well . . . you know. Anyway, if nobody eats leftovers, stop making left-overs. Worst case, you'll underestimate people's appetites and have to add a slice of bread on the side or have a snack later. No biggie.
- And maybe most importantly: Let some things run out. I grew up in a house that had backups of everything and let me tell you . . . the amount of past-date food we ate. If you're ballin' and it helps you sleep at night to go stock that extra ketchup, have at 'er. But in my house it's pretty normal to go a couple days without some ingredients between shops, and nobody has ever starved. Letting things run out forces you to get creative and use up things you haven't been reaching for.

SHOP SMARTER

The chart on page 21 visually explains how I try to spend my money when grocery shopping, with the approximate percent of my budget I allocate to each quadrant. Of course these percentages vary from week to week based on what I need and store sales, but overall my decision-making process remains the same: I prioritize mostly items in the low-cost, high-nutrition quadrant. These are the basic ingredients that are pretty much always affordable, as well as produce and meats that are on a good sale (because as we know, just because it's on sale doesn't mean it's a good deal) and will fill you up or help you meet nutritional goals. Think grains like rice and oats; root vegetables like potatoes and carrots; frozen vegetables; lower-cost or in-season fruits such as bananas and apples; proteins like beans, lentils, and, depending on the sale, bone-in chicken, canned tuna, and nut butters.

Grocery flyers and signs will usually try to make things look like a good deal, but whether or not it's a good value is for the customer to evaluate. Start familiarizing yourself with value by looking at the price per weight, which is usually in small print just below the dollar amount on the price sign.

I spend a bit in the low-cost/low-nutrition quadrant as well as in the high-cost/high-nutrition quadrant (especially if these are items I really like and they are on sale). Low-cost/low-nutrition are things like store-brand potato chips or the baked goods my store marks down to half price when they are near their sell-by date.

High-cost/high-nutrition are the straw-berries my daughter requests, which I buy regardless of the price because the girl will eat only two kinds of fruit. Or sometimes you just need butter or olive oil because you ran out and who knows when the next sale will be. I try to limit the number of items I buy "regardless of the price"; there's always *something* else we would be perfectly happy to eat, but grocery shopping shouldn't mentally break you or take three hours, so just try to factor a little buffer into your budget for decision fatigue.

I try to avoid the high-cost/low-nutrition quadrant but do allow some purchases here—consider them "joy points." If something brings you enough joy to be worth the high cost, then factor it into your budget! Even then I will try to choose something not astronomical—for example, I'll treat us to some of our favorite snacks for movie night, but I'll choose the chip or candy brands that are having a multi-deal sale. We also love trying new foods and

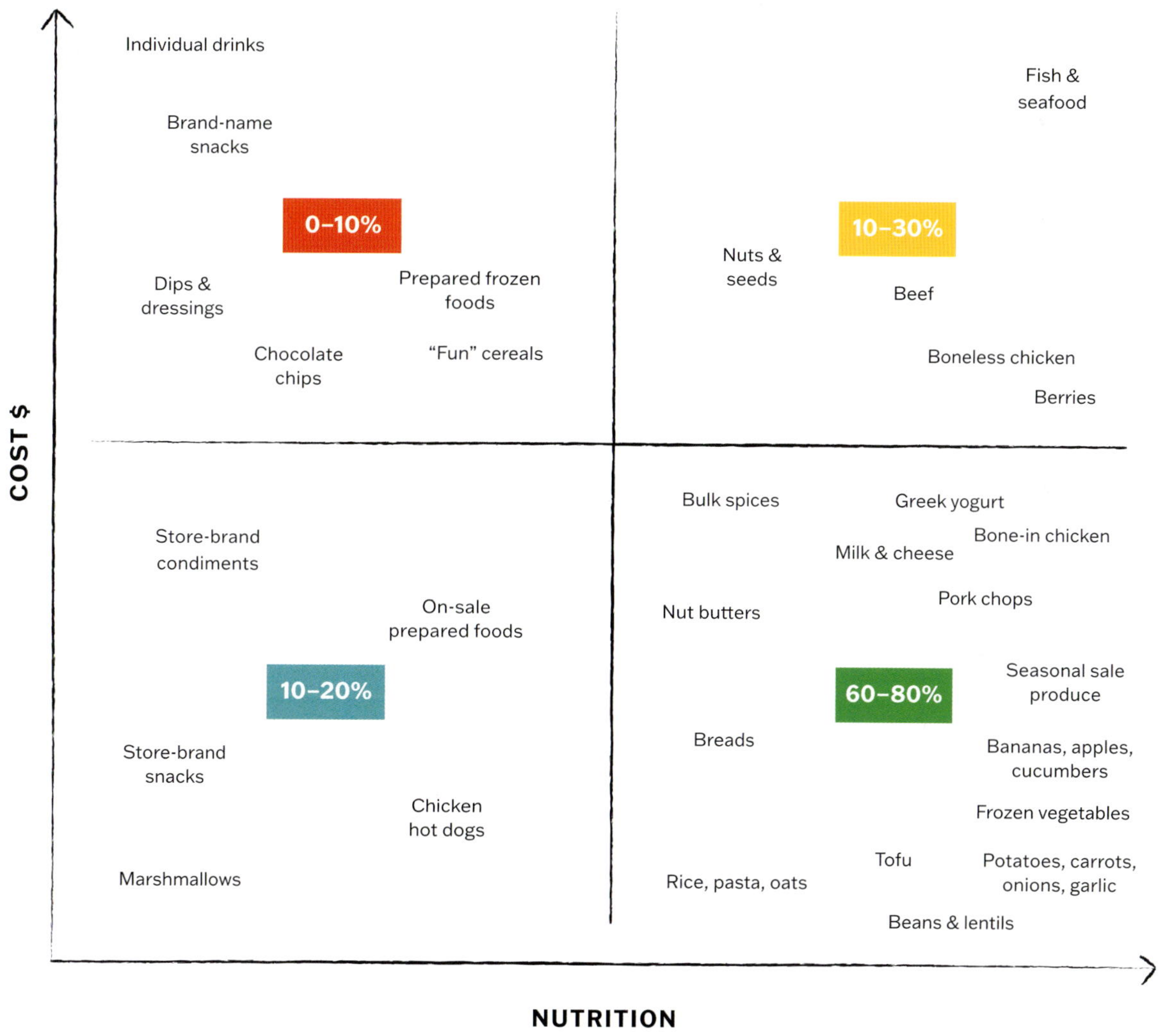

sometimes that *is* the activity. Paying $6 for a single dragon fruit once a year just for the experience is A-OK with me. Which leads me to . . .

- You're allowed to have nice things, but you don't need all the nice things—and neither do your kids. Obviously if you're dealing with special circumstances or medical concerns, this one is not for you, so consult your medical professional. Food is joy, and you should treat yourself to some of your favorite things. Heck, if money isn't a concern, treat yourself to all of them . . . but for most of us trying to stay on budget, that's just not realistic. When I notice my kids' favorite snacks are on sale, I will get a few, and other weeks they get the snacks that are on sale that week (that they still do like). Some weeks grapes are a good price; other weeks we get apples. And we have lots of other foods to eat down a bit before I get groceries again, so we all understand that if we run through all the snacks on day 1, on days 2 through 7 we'll have to fill up on what's left.
- Skip the top-up shops. If you're anything like me, going to the store for two ingredients turns into grabbing ten more on impulse because "I'm here anyway" or "It's a good sale" and now you're walking around with your arms at max capacity and $100 less in your bank account.
- Stop paying full price for everything. Try to get familiar with what's actually a good price per weight or item in your area by watching the flyers over a few weeks or months. Store brands have also come a long way. I recommend downloading a grocery flyer app, which consolidates your local sales in one place and is searchable so you can choose a store with the best prices on items you want. Two apps I use regularly are Flipp for reviewing local flyers and Flashfood, where stores can post near-date items, typically for half price. It's not uncommon for me to change my meal plan on the fly in the store because I don't like the price of an item. I shop sales and marked-down items, and my eyes are always peeled for a deal. I'm able to do this because my cooking skills (and pantry basics—I go over this more on page 35) allow me to make something delicious out of whatever I have available to me.

LEARN TO COOK

Once you accept that it's not that deep—it's just dinner—the second part of your life begins. There are some basic techniques that every home cook should know, which you'll find in "Methods Made Easy" (page 35).

- Start using recipes as guides instead of rule books (that's why I created this cookbook, by the way!). You don't need every ingredient, and it takes only 30 seconds to look up a substitution (check out my tables for common swaps on page 28). I promise you won't ruin the recipe if you replace one missing or too-expensive ingredient (thoughtfully of course) or even skip it altogether.
- Don't be afraid to season! And don't be scared off by the long spice lists in my recipes! Seasoning is an easy and affordable way to elevate your food. I recommend adding one or two spices to each grocery order until you build up

a collection, and using them freely. See more on spices in on pages 24 to 27.

- Shop your kitchen first. I know it's tempting to make all those recipes you saved while scrolling. But just as you don't need a whole new wardrobe every season, you can add one or two new and exciting recipes to your cart per week and build the rest of your meal plan around what you already have. In manufacturing we call this FIFO (first in, first out), which also helps reduce waste. Figuring out what to make with what you have can seem daunting at first, but I gotchu—check out my "What Do You Need to Do?" flowchart (page 41) for some super flexible recipes.
- But still keep a few convenience items on hand! Sometimes the day goes sideways or you just don't have it in you to cook, and that frozen pizza or boxed mac and cheese will save you from spending much more on takeout.

Most importantly—get help if you need it. There's no shame in using your local food pantry or community kitchen. If you're experiencing food insecurity, please find local resources and use them. You deserve nourishment. Period.

FOLLOW FOOD SAFETY GUIDELINES

My rule of thumb with leftovers is two to four days if refrigerated properly. Vegetables that are a little wrinkly and less firm are just dehydrated and still safe to use, but if anything is moldy, slimy, or overly soft, it's time to toss it. If you see small spots on firm produce, you can cut off 1 inch (2.5 cm) all the way around and still use the rest. When in doubt, refer to food safety guidelines.

BUT REALLY, TELL ME WHAT TO BUY

WHAT I STOCK IN MY KITCHEN SO I CAN USE WHAT I HAVE

I'm all about substituting ingredients instead of running to the store, but every meal has to start somewhere. If I were stocking my kitchen from scratch, here are the 30 ingredients I'd keep on hand to make cooking on the fly easier (plus a lot of spices, which I'll talk about next). These are the ones you'll see come up again and again in my recipes. I stand behind this: You need some things, but you don't need all the things. For example, I might have olive oil and canola oil but not avocado or coconut oil. Honestly,

KEY INGREDIENT	WHAT I USUALLY CHOOSE
Baking soda, baking powder	Baking soda
Beans and lentils	Black beans, white kidney beans (cannellini), brown or red lentils
Bouillon or broth	Chicken bouillon
Breading materials	Panko or crackers
Cheese	Mozzarella, cheddar
Coating and thickening	Cornstarch
Condensed soups	Cream of mushroom, tomato
Eggs	Large, from chickens
Flour	All-purpose
Fluid dairy	Cow's milk, plain Greek yogurt
Garlic	Fresh or powder
Mayonnaise	Real mayo
Meats	Bone-in chicken thighs, pork chops, ground beef
Mustard	Dijon
Nut butter	Peanut butter
Oats	Quick oats
Oil	Canola (vegetable) or olive
Onions	Fresh or powder
Pasta	Any, mix it up
Potatoes	Yellow or red (personal preference)
Rice	Basmati or parboiled
Soy sauce	Low-sodium
Spices and herbs	Garlic powder, onion powder, oregano, smoked paprika, salt, and pepper (but try to collect more)

KEY INGREDIENT	WHAT I USUALLY CHOOSE
Sweeteners	White sugar, honey
Tofu	Extra-firm
Tomatoes, paste, and sauce	Tomato paste
Tuna	Chunk, packed in water
Vanilla	Real, in bulk
Vegetables	Carrots, lettuce, frozen vegetables
Vinegar	Apple cider vinegar

which one I choose on any given shopping trip is 50 percent price, 50 percent vibes, but if I'm only getting one it'll always be the most versatile . . . unless there's a sale, of course. ;)

HOW I BUY AND STORE MY SPICES

I cannot recommend enough to build a collection of spices and use them freely. In my videos you'll often see me pull out a clear bin full of zipper-top spice bags. This is the format I buy most often as the store brands where I live come this way, but you can also often find more affordable brands of spices in the international aisle, and large shakers at bulk stores. More spices, lower cost, no brainer.

I like keeping mine in a bin that I can easily pull out and flip through like a Rolodex (no, they aren't sorted alphabetically, although that would be a great way to organize them). People often comment that I should put them in shakers or jars and the reality is that at the rate I use them I'd be giving myself a maintenance job I just don't want. Plus, I have no interest in shuffling through 20 tiny jars in a cupboard, knocking half of them over every time. If you already have tiny jars I recommend labeling the tops and putting them in a bin you can pull out when you cook (or dedicate a drawer to spices if you have space).

MAKING FOOD WITH THE WRONG INGREDIENTS

FLAVOR PROFILES EXPLAINED

A few years ago, my mom called me and asked, "Alex, how do you know what spices go with what? How do you know what works and what doesn't?" That was the day I realized that substituting and cooking without recipes is a learned skill—one I learned without noticing.

So where do we start? Every culture has actually already done a lot of the legwork for you. If you look at different cuisines, you'll notice they reuse a lot of the same ingredients and flavors across recipes.

Italian food has herbs, tomatoes, pasta. Indian food has curry, lentils, rice. Mexican food has corn, beans, cumin. You get the point. The more spices you have in your cabinet, the easier it will be to be free in the kitchen.

While this is in no way an exhaustive list, you can consider this a quick "cheat sheet" of some core combinations of ingredients that are generally accessible and go well together to get you started. Cultural cuisines are more nuanced and complex than this book will get into, so if you love a specific cuisine, I recommend finding a cookbook on it to learn more.

GREEK: lemon, oregano, garlic, olive oil, mint, yogurt

FRENCH: butter, cream, fines herbes, Dijon mustard, red wine, tomato sauce

CARIBBEAN: jerk seasoning, citrus, hot peppers, garlic, allspice, thyme

THAI: fish sauce, lime, chilies, coconut milk, cilantro, green or red curry paste

CHINESE: soy sauce, garlic, ginger, sesame oil, vinegar, brown sugar
INDIAN: yogurt, yellow curry powder, garam masala, garlic, ginger, coconut milk
MEXICAN: cumin, cilantro, garlic, onion, lime, jalapeño/habanero
ITALIAN: tomato sauce, Italian seasoning, garlic, balsamic vinegar, olive oil, Parmesan cheese

Fusion cuisine has become more popular in recent decades, so once you're comfortable, start mixing it up! Worse case you eat a mediocre meal and try again next time, but best case you nail it and gain some confidence in the kitchen. And remember, it's not that deep, it's just dinner.

BALANCING FLAVORS: HOW TO FIX A RECIPE

If you're going rogue on a recipe, the biggest thing you need to consider is balancing flavors. There's a reason you don't put raisins in your beef and broccoli, but you're able to get away with cabbage. Keeping your swaps "in the family" will ensure your meal turns out at worst OK but very likely much better.

If you think of your meal like a scale, if you remove something from one side you wouldn't then put it on the other side to make it balance. Here are some opposing flavors and examples so you can start balancing your dishes by taste, keeping in mind that sometimes you'll also have to increase a second element to balance what you used to balance.

ACID/SOURNESS → SWEETNESS

- If your spaghetti sauce is too acidic, add a teaspoon of sugar at a time. Let it simmer for a few minutes for the flavors to meld, then taste and add more if needed.
- If your salad dressing is too tart (from vinegar or lemon juice), try adding a tablespoon of honey. You may also end up needing more salt; sometimes balancing is three-dimensional.

SWEETNESS → SALTINESS

- Most desserts need a pinch of salt so they don't turn out sickly sweet.
- If you oversweetened your spaghetti sauce (this is why I recommend adding slowly), adding a bit more salt may help correct it.

BITTERNESS → SALTINESS

- Seasoning cruciferous vegetables like cabbage and broccoli with salt when roasting helps balance the bitterness.

SPICINESS → FAT OR SWEETNESS

- You've probably heard that drinking milk will tame the heat in your mouth better than water. Similarly, if you've added too many red pepper flakes to your tomato sauce, try adding cheese or turn it into a pink sauce with cream to mellow the flavor.
- If your stir-fry is too spicy, adding a bit of sugar or honey may help—you may also decide to increase the acidity with a bit of vinegar to balance the extra sweetness.

SALTINESS → IT DEPENDS

- If you accidentally poured too much and it's still on top, try to scoop it out or rinse solid ingredients under water.
- Add a potato, rice, or more unsalted broth to a pot of soup to dilute it. You'll end up with a bigger dish, so the proportion of salt per bite will be less.

- Try adding more sweetness or acidic ingredients to cut the salt.
- Ultimately, if you've made the dish inedible, it may be worth cutting your losses rather than adding more ingredients. Sometimes you can also portion out part of the dish and add to just that part.

One thing about salt is you can always add more but you can't take it out. How much salt to put in a recipe is tricky because everyone's palate is different, plus your tastes change over time and based on your general diet. If you eat a lot of takeout and packaged foods or even use a lot of prepared sauces and seasonings in your home cooking, you're probably accustomed to a saltier flavor profile. In contrast, when my kids were babies our palates got adjusted to unsalted food since added salt should be limited before age two. Because of this variance, I usually err on the side of caution and use less salt in my recipes; this way each person can decide if they want to add extra salt to their plate.

SUBS SUBS SUBS

The quickest way to rack up your grocery bill unnecessarily is adding those one-off ingredients you'll never use again from that one recipe on your list. And don't even get me started on running to the store for every missing ingredient. I'll *always* end up buying more than I went in for. Plus, even if you live steps from the store, finding the item and checking out still takes longer than googling a swap.

The truth is, you probably already have something that will do the trick at home. Will it be exactly the same? Maybe, maybe not. Will it be close enough that the average person wouldn't know the difference? Probably. Will you ruin the recipe is you use a tablespoon of apple cider vinegar instead of rice vinegar? Absolutely not. Anyway, here are some common subs to save you time, money, and your sanity at dinner time.

NEED THIS?	TRY THIS
Baking powder	Baking soda (half as much)
Bouillon	Salt + onion powder + garlic powder
Bread crumbs	Crackers, oats
Broth	Bouillon + water
Brown sugar	White sugar + molasses
Butter	For melting: margarine or neutral oil For spreading: whip refined coconut oil, nutritional yeast + salt
Buttermilk	Milk + lemon juice or vinegar

NEED THIS?	TRY THIS
Chicken	Extra-firm tofu, pork chops Chickpeas + bouillon or extra seasoning
Citrus juice	Vinegar + sugar, other juice
Condensed cream soups	Roux (butter + flour + milk), seasoned as desired
Cottage cheese, ricotta cheese	In eggs and dips: Greek yogurt In lasagna and casseroles: mozzarella
Egg (for baking)	1 tablespoon ground flax + 3 tablespoons water Aquafaba (liquid from canned chickpeas)
Fish sauce	Soy sauce
Fresh herbs	Dried herbs (one-third as much)
Garlic cloves	Garlic powder, jarred garlic
Ground beef	Brown lentils
Heavy cream	Milk + melted butter
Honey	Maple syrup, sugar
Ketchup	Tomato paste + vinegar + sugar + water
Lemon juice	Vinegar (half as much)
Mayonnaise	Plain yogurt
Mushrooms (for texture and bulking)	Eggplant, tofu, brown lentils
Nut butters (school-safe)	Honestly none of them will be as good, but try sun butter, Wow Butter, or chickpea butter
Oil or melted butter (for baking)	Applesauce, mashed banana, yogurt
Onions	Onion powder, shallots, green onions. If due to allergy: celery, bell peppers (will change flavor)
Parmesan cheese	Blend raw cashews + nutritional yeast + garlic powder + salt (won't melt, good for topping)
Pork	Beef, chicken
Quinoa	Rice, couscous
Red wine vinegar	Balsamic vinegar + apple cider vinegar
Rice vinegar	Apple cider vinegar

NEED THIS?	TRY THIS
Sausage	Ground: lentils Links: paneer
Sour cream	Greek yogurt
Soy sauce	Straight sub: tamari. You can sub soy sauce for something salty (bouillon, for example) in some recipes, like a marinade or BBQ sauce. In Asian recipes where it's a major part of the flavor profile, you should probably just find another recipe to make tonight.
Sweet potato	Squash
Tomato sauce	Tomato paste + water
Wheat flour	1:1 gluten-free flour, blended oats (will be denser)
Wine, red	Balsamic vinegar + sugar + water; vinegar + red juice (such as cranberry)
Wine, white	Vinegar + apple juice; vinegar + sugar + water
Worcestershire sauce	Soy sauce + sugar or juice

USE MORE SPICES!

Spices are my favorite easy and affordable way to elevate a dish! I highly recommend building your collection by adding one or two spices to every grocery order until you have a good stash (for more on how I buy and store spices, see page 25). But my pantry wasn't built in a day, and I don't expect you to have everything (duh!), so here are some spice-specific subs you can use in the meantime:

NEED THIS?	TRY THIS
Allspice	Cinnamon + ginger + cloves
Cinnamon	Nutmeg (start with one-quarter as much) or allspice
Curry powder	Garam masala, or cumin + coriander + turmeric
Ground ginger	Allspice
Herbs: basil, oregano, thyme, rosemary, parsley	Use just one or a mix or the others.
Italian seasoning	Rosemary, thyme, basil, oregano, parsley
Old Bay seasoning or Cajun seasoning	Chili powder, paprika, garlic powder, onion powder, thyme, salt, pepper + cayenne
Smoked paprika	Chili powder or paprika
Summer savory	Marjoram + thyme + oregano
Taco seasoning	Chili powder, cumin, paprika, oregano, garlic powder, onion powder, salt + pepper
Turmeric	Omit (dish won't be yellow)

KITCHEN SMALL APPLIANCES & TOOLS

I think we all know we need pots, pans, knives, a cutting board, spatulas, etc. to cook, but here are some things beyond the bare basics I use regularly, and if you're cooking a lot, you may want to consider.

APPLIANCES

INSTANT POT OR ELECTRIC PRESSURE COOKER

Everything you make in the electric pressure cooker can be done in a Dutch oven, but if you like to set it and forget it, this one is for you.

HOT TIPS

1. A 6-quart machine needs 1 cup liquid to pressurize—check your manual for other sizes.

FOOD	COOK TIME (ON HIGH)	RELEASE	NOTES
RICE	5 minutes	Natural	Equal parts rice + water
EGGS	3 minutes for soft 4 minutes for medium 5 minutes for hard	3 minutes natural, then quick	Ice bath for 5 minutes stops them overcooking
POTATOES, CUBED	8 minutes	Natural	
PASTA	4 minutes	Quick	1 pound (454 g) pasta + 4 cups water

2. This appliance heats liquid to a steam that creates the pressure needed to cook. If your liquid is thick it can't turn into steam. But it'll keep heating and trying, and, you're gonna end up with a burn notice—so don't stir before you set it!

3. The size of the food piece(s) dictates the cook time, regardless of the number of pieces. I often have to look up cook times, but here's a table with some I frequently use:

SLOW COOKER

The Instant Pot slow cooker function leaves a lot to be desired. Unfortunately, if you want to use both, you'll need to have both. But it's pretty nice to dump in some ingredients and come home to a meal.

HOT TIP: Unlike in a pressure cooker, you don't need to add liquid to a slow cooker. If every slow cooker meal you make turns into mush, try skipping the added liquid (meat and veggies will release some liquid anyhow).

Slow cooking from frozen is a controversial topic, and you should always refer to your machine's instruction manual. The concern is food staying in an unsafe temperature zone for too long (over 2 hours). It can create the perfect environment to harbor bacteria that could make you sick. The Crock-Pot brand does give the green light on their website, as it heats quicker and hotter than some other brands. If you are going to cook meat from frozen, always set the slow cooker to high heat and cook a smaller amount of food that was frozen flat; avoid large blocks that won't be able to come to a safe temperature quickly.

BLENDER

Honestly, if you're not making smoothies, I'd probably opt for a food processor because it can do more things. They are somewhat interchangeable, and I don't think you need both. If you are making smoothies, it's worth reading reviews and investing in a higher-end blender. Some blend smoother and handle ice better than others.

MINI FOOD PROCESSOR

This is nice to have for when you don't feel like dicing and mincing. I'm all about shaving time off my prep, and I'm not a big enough perfectionist to care whether my veggies are cubed or my cheese is crumbled instead of grated—it all melts the same. It's also great to puree ingredients if you're trying to hide them. And the bowl, top, and blade can even go in the dishwasher.

AIR FRYER

This is a mini convection oven. People love them because they heat up fast and cook fast, and there are a few things they do a bit better than a full-sized oven, like cooking frozen French fries, or my Midnight Crispy Chicken Thighs (page 45). If you're cooking for one or two, I totally get the hype, but I have yet to find one that's big enough to cook a whole meal for my family (and mine is an XL). For me it's a nice-to-have for quick lunches but not a must-have if you have access to an oven. This is the basic recipe conversion from oven to air fryer: Reduce the oven temperature by 25 to 50°F (20°C) and reduce the cook time by 20 to 25 percent.

TOOLS

MEAT THERMOMETER

If you're a parent, you've probably heard the saying "Watch the baby, not the clock." Same applies in cooking—all ovens aren't the same, nor is every piece of meat. Recipes give approximate times, but a thermometer takes all the guesswork out of "Is it done?" And it's not just for meat—bread is done at 210°F (100°C), and you don't have to stick your finger in the casserole to see if it's heated through anymore.

ROTARY GRATER

I was a late adopter on this one and I still don't take it out for every meal, but I do like being able to easily grate potatoes or thinly slice a whole cucumber without slicing my fingers. As a home cook, I'd personally choose this over a mandoline. But there's nothing this does that you can't do with a box grater and a knife, so if you're tight on money or space, it's more of a nice-to-have, depending on what you're cooking.

KNIFE SHARPENER

Because sharp knives are easier and safer to work with, a sharpener is nonnegotiable. I have a three-stage knife sharpener that is super easy to use. Does it give professional results? Who knows. But it does the job and requires zero training.

MEAT MASHER

This is a convenience thing, but it's just so much easier than breaking ground meat apart with a spatula. It's also great for shredding pulled meat quickly.

FINE-MESH STRAINER

For draining and rinsing your beans and lentils. A regular strainer or colander will do in a pinch, but smaller stuff tends to fall through the holes so I like to have both. It can be a bit of a pain to wash if you let stuff get dried on, so always at a minimum give it a good spray immediately after using.

PARCHMENT PAPER

Having to soak and scrub pans is enough to make me not want to cook the meal. Eliminate unnecessary mental roadblocks and just buy the parchment paper.

KITCHEN MATH (WORK SMARTER NOT HARDER)

Nothing scratches that baking itch like a recipe that uses the same measuring spoon or cup over and over. Those recipes are few and far between, but with a little mental math you can cut your dishes down by half or more. I've also included a column for quick reference when halving recipes because sometimes you just don't want a family-size meal.

MEASUREMENT	CONVERTS TO	HALF-MEASURE
1 tablespoon	3 teaspoons	½ tablespoon or 1½ teaspoons
⅛ cup	2 tablespoons	1 tablespoon
¼ cup	4 tablespoons	2 tablespoons
⅓ cup	5 tablespoons + 1 teaspoon	2 tablespoons + 2 teaspoons (or round up to 3 tablespoons)
½ cup	8 tablespoons	¼ cup
⅔ cup	2 × ⅓ cup or ½ cup + 2½ tablespoons	⅓ cup
¾ cup	3 × ¼ cup or 12 tablespoons	¼ cup + 2 tablespoons
1 cup	2 × ½ cup	½ cup
1½ cups	2 × ¾ cup	¾ cup or ½ cup + ¼ cup
1¾ cups	7 × ¾ cup	¾ cup + 2 tablespoons
1 quart or 1 L	4 cups	2 cups
1 gallon	16 cups or 4 L	8 cups or 2 L

METHODS MADE EASY

If you're a beginner cook, every meal can feel overwhelming. What's the difference between sear, brown, and sauté? How to I make a roux and what is it? Don't let the terminology scare you away, as there are only a handful of basic methods you'll actually end up using regularly. The fancy stuff you see in cooking shows is cool but not required to make 99 percent of everyday meals. I'm not a trained chef, just a home cook who figured out what works by trial and error—and I'm here to break it down, the easy way.

CHOPPING

Vegetables are round, so they are gonna rock and roll. Don't make the task harder—cut them in half to make a flat surface, then put that flat side face down. Now you're not working with a moving target and much less likely to cut yourself.

If you're looking to speed up your slicing, I've found that rocking the knife blade back and forth in one spot and slowly guiding the food toward the knife is most efficient. If you've ever seen a mandoline used, you can probably picture what I mean. And on that note—curl your fingers under, because nothing ruins the cooking mood like slicing your finger.

CUTTING MEAT AGAINST THE GRAIN

Honestly, this one is tricky because meat isn't uniform, but basically imagine it like the cuff on a sweatshirt. Pull toward your hand and there's no give, but pull around your wrist and it stretches. Visually with a cuff you can see the ribbing, so it's obvious which way it will stretch. Sometimes on meat you can see the "grain" (that is, the fibers), and you want to cut perpendicular to that. If you can't see it, try to find the stretchy side and cut perpendicular to that. When you cut against the grain, you're shortening the fibers of the meat, making it less tough to chew through. Typically, if you're getting a thinner cut, like a steak, the butcher already did this for you.

SEARING VERSUS BROWNING

The whole point of searing meat is to seal the cut and keep the juices in. They really should have called it sealing, and all you have to do is turn up the heat (medium-high should do) and cook every side of the meat to have a brown crust on it, usually a couple minutes per side. Yes, meat gets brown when you sear it, but browning is more used to talk about ground meat, and what they mean by this is to cook it through. This is a food safety thing—when the outer layer of a cut of meat is exposed to air, it creates opportunity for bacteria to enter. Ground meat is basically all outer layer, so you need to cook it all, whereas a steak can be a little pink inside because the middle wasn't exposed to air.

COOKING TEMPERATURES

BTW, while we're on the topic of cooking temps, here are some general food-safe temperatures for meat. Insert a meat thermometer into the center of the cut, and don't let the thermometer go through to the pan or into the air or you won't get an accurate reading.

MARINADES & BRINES

Let's take a cheap cut of meat—and make it better! Marinades and brines are the ultimate cheap meat hack, so here's the what, why, and how to wing it.

Brines are mostly water and salt, intended to make poultry or pork more tender and juicier. The ratio I use is about 3 tablespoons salt for every 4 cups water, and you'll want to soak boneless chicken or pork chops for about 1 hour, bone-in for up to 2, and whole chickens for 4 to 6. To take it a step further, add sugar, lemon juice or vinegar, and herbs and spices. Always brine in the refrigerator—food safety first! After

MEAT	TEMPERATURE
Poultry	165°F (74°C); if bone-in, insert in thickest part of meat, avoiding the bone (bone conducts heat differently and will give a false reading)
Pork	145°F (63°C); I don't trust pink pork (for no good reason), so I still use 165°F (74°C)
Beef	Ground beef: 165°F (74°C) Steak or roast to medium: 145°F (63°C)
Fish	145°F (63°C) for most fish

brining, pat the meat dry with a paper towel before cooking.

HOT TIP: When I've forgotten to thaw meat, sometimes I'll soak it in a brine in the refrigerator. Thawing in cold water is faster than thawing in nothing—but if I'm going to waterlog my meat, I may as well be intentional and give it some flavor!

Brines are not intended to be left "up to overnight"—if you need more time, that's where marinades come in . . .

Marinades are a great way to pump flavor into meat. You'll want to marinate pieces for a minimum of 1 hour, but you can always leave it longer. I like to use a combination of salt, acid, sweet (not too much—sugar can burn), and oil, plus some flavor boosters. Since the flavor is more intense, you won't need nearly as much liquid as with a brine. The easiest way to marinate is in a zipper-top bag so the meat gets coated, but you can also do it in a mixing bowl or covered casserole dish, and you'll want to flip the pieces halfway through so both sides absorb the marinade.

HOT TIP: I love portioning and freezing meat right in the marinade—by the time it thaws, it's ready to cook with no extra prep!

Here are some easy marinade ingredients you probably already have on hand:

SALTY	SWEET	ACIDIC	EXTRA
Soy sauce	Honey	Vinegar	Herbs
Broth	Maple syrup	Lemon juice	Spices
Salt water	Sugar	Mustard	Oil

ROUX & GRAVY

These are essentially the same recipes with different ingredients. You need a fat, a thickener, and a liquid (plus flavor). For a roux, melt a few tablespoons of butter in a saucepan over low heat. Mix in an equal amount of flour and cook for a minute, then whisk in some milk or cream. Start slowly, let it thicken (this happens automatically after a couple minutes), and then add more milk to reach the desired thickness.

Here's where it gets neat—you can season with salt and pepper and call it a day, but melt in a couple handfuls of grated cheddar and you have cheese sauce. Or start with sautéed mushrooms and you have homemade condensed mushroom soup.

Gravy uses fat from a roast as the base instead of butter. My MIL makes the best gravy, so I'm sharing her method: Mix together some flour and cold water and whisk into the hot roast drippings. Again, start with less water since you can always add more later to thin it out. Season with salt and pepper (and garlic powder if you're into it). Keep stirring for a few minutes as the gravy thickens.

MIREPOIX

Pronounced "meer-pwah," this is a classic French cooking base made up of chopped onion, celery, and carrot. Mirepoix is the base for many soups, stews, and sauces, which is why you often see those three ingredients listed in recipes. Sometimes you can even find frozen mirepoix mix or a frozen chopped vegetable mix called spaghetti vegetables—this one often also contains bell peppers, which may or may not suit your recipe. Typically, the ratio for mirepoix is 2 parts onion to 1 part each celery and carrot. The vegetables are sautéed in fat such as butter or oil, and the purpose is to "sweat" them to release flavor, not to caramelize them—so keep the heat medium-low to medium and stir often.

HOW TO MICROWAVE FROZEN VEGETABLES

Sometimes I get halfway through a recipe and feel myself getting anxious. This is usually on nights when we are either in a rush to get to the kids' activities or I haven't taken care of myself and waited too long to eat. On those nights I say, NOT EVERYTHING HAS TO BE A RECIPE! My kids are perfectly happy to eat a side of frozen veggies. Here's how to make them in the microwave when you just can't tonight:

Pour a couple cups of frozen vegetables into a microwave-safe bowl. Top with a pat of butter and microwave on high for 3 to 5 minutes (3 minutes for peas, corn, etc., 5 for larger veggies like broccoli). Stir in the butter and salt to taste. I used to add water and drain it until someone on TikTok told me you don't have to—life-changing enough for me to include it in this book. You're welcome.

THERE'S NOTHING TO EAT IN THIS HOUSE! BUT WE USE WHAT WE HAVE . . .

Nothing jazzes me up more than a good round of *Chopped* at home! Give me a pile of odds and ends and I'll give you a gourmet-ish meal (or at least a cohesive one). And those leftovers nobody's reaching for? Makeover time. Food waste is the quickest way to rack up a high grocery bill.

But if your creative brain isn't firing at the sight of your need-to-use-now random pantry-ingredient collab, here's a flowchart to help you figure out which of my foolproof flexible meals to make tonight. Pick one of these recipes when you just can't bear to eat those left-overs again or when you're trying to stretch it another couple of days before getting groceries. Some of these recipes contain meat, others don't, and they can all be added or subtracted—that's the whole point of using what you have! If you need some more help with substitutions, pop over to page 28 for a handy table.

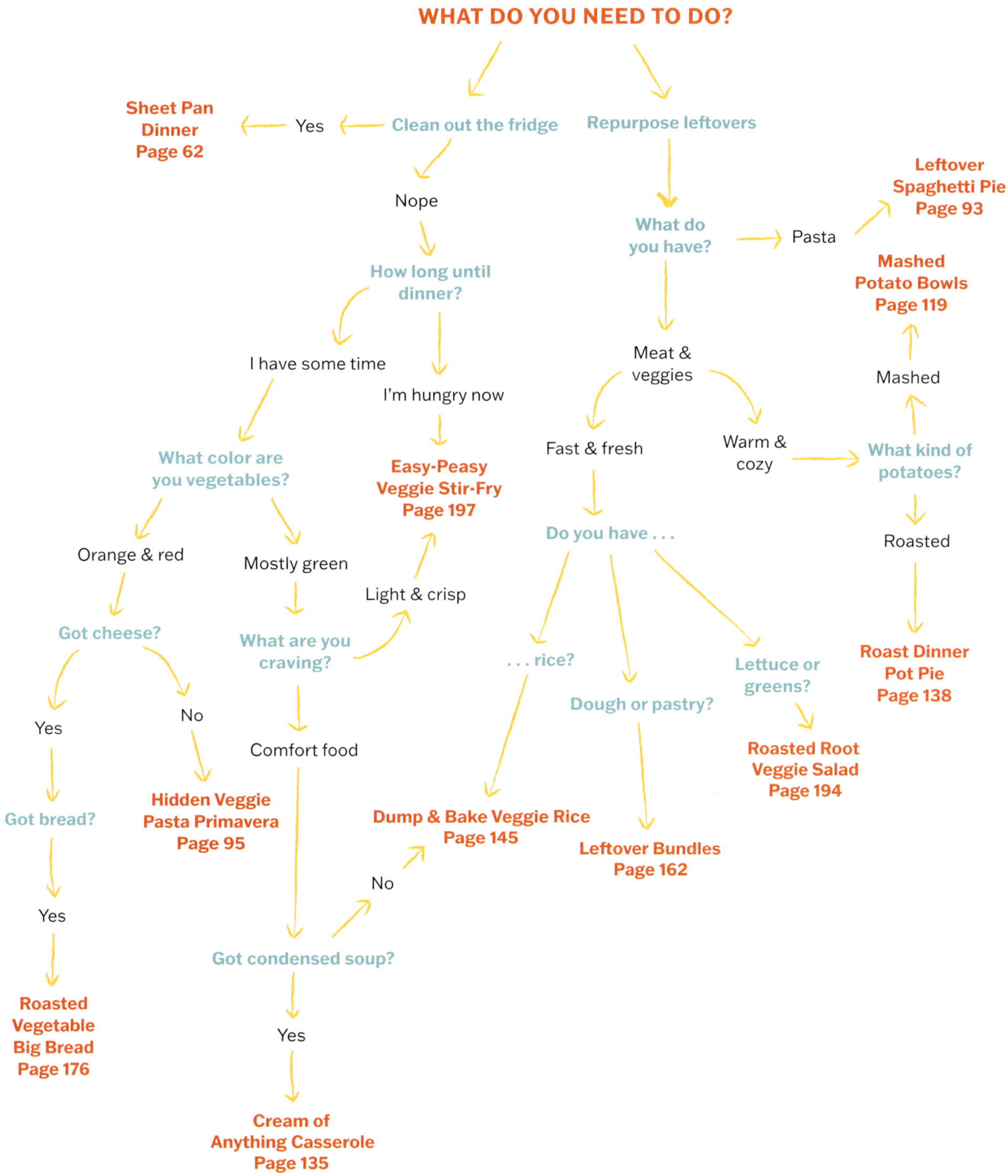
WHAT DO YOU NEED TO DO?
Clean out the fridge
Repurpose leftovers
Yes
Sheet Pan Dinner Page 62
Nope
How long until dinner?
I have some time
I'm hungry now
Easy-Peasy Veggie Stir-Fry Page 197
What color are you vegetables?
Orange & red
Mostly green
Got cheese?
Yes
No
Hidden Veggie Pasta Primavera Page 95
Got bread?
Yes
Roasted Vegetable Big Bread Page 176
What are you craving?
Light & crisp
Comfort food
Got condensed soup?
No
Dump & Bake Veggie Rice Page 145
Yes
Cream of Anything Casserole Page 135
What do you have?
Pasta
Leftover Spaghetti Pie Page 93
Meat & veggies
Fast & fresh
Warm & cozy
What kind of potatoes?
Mashed
Mashed Potato Bowls Page 119
Roasted
Roast Dinner Pot Pie Page 138
Do you have . . .
. . . rice?
Dough or pastry?
Leftover Bundles Page 162
Lettuce or greens?
Roasted Root Veggie Salad Page 194

CHAPTER ONE

FOR THE LOVE OF MEAT & POTATOES (. . . OR RICE)

The recipes in this chapter use more affordable cuts of meat because let's be real, when you're trying to feed yourself or your family on a typical weeknight (and probably on a budget), you're not out here looking for how to cook filet mignon. But we also use what we have in terms of energy, and at the end of a long day there's something about a simple three-component meal that just feels done like dinner. Choose your own sides (check out chapter 6, Salads & Veggies, for ideas) or pair with the ones I've recommended in the headnotes.

MIDNIGHT CRISPY CHICKEN THIGHS

SERVES 4 TO 6

- ¼ cup (60 mL) mayonnaise
- 2 teaspoons garlic powder
- 2 teaspoons onion powder
- 2 teaspoons paprika
- 1 teaspoon dried parsley
- ½ teaspoon salt
- ¼ teaspoon pepper
- 2 pounds (1 kg) bone-in, skin-on chicken thighs
- 2 cups (100 g) panko breadcrumbs

I made these on a whim one night when I realized I had forgotten to cook the family-size pack of chicken thighs I had thawed. It was a use-it-or-lose-it situation, but they turned out SO GOOD! It's simple, and satisfies that crispy fried chicken craving without the mess of frying.

To say these are baked is a bit misleading because they turn out best in the air fryer, but you can also use the convection setting on your oven, or just cook for an extra 5 to 10 minutes in a regular oven.

---

1. Preheat an air fryer or convection oven to 400°F (200°C). Line a large rimmed baking sheet with parchment paper if using the oven.
2. Mix together the mayonnaise and seasonings in a large bowl. Pat the chicken dry with a paper towel, then place in the bowl and massage the sauce all over the chicken with your hands to coat.
3. Pour the panko into a shallow bowl and roll the chicken thighs in the crumbs, then place in the air fryer basket or on the lined baking sheet. Air-fry or bake for 15 to 20 minutes, or until a meat thermometer inserted reaches at least 165°F (74°C) and the chicken is golden and crispy. Check the temperature on a few pieces to be sure they are cooked through. Allow the chicken to rest for a few minutes before serving.

CHICKEN DON'T HURRY

SERVES 4 TO 6

2 pounds (1 kg) chicken legs, skin removed if desired

½ cup (125 mL) ketchup

¼ cup (60 g) brown sugar

¼ cup (60 mL) water

1 tablespoon onion powder

2 teaspoons beef bouillon

1 teaspoons garlic powder

1 teaspoon Worcestershire sauce

Chicken hurry was one of my mom's staples for years. Back then she baked chicken breasts in ketchup and dried onion soup mix. My version with chicken legs is more affordable (but you can use breasts if you prefer). Plus, you don't need to buy a packet of onion soup mix because the ingredients are probably already in your pantry. Serve over white rice with boiled carrots and a slice of buttered bread on the side for a super easy '90s-inspired meal.

1. Grease a slow cooker insert with nonstick cooking spray and add the chicken.
2. Mix together the ketchup, brown sugar, water, onion powder, bouillon, garlic powder, and Worcestershire in a small bowl and pour over the chicken. Cover and cook on low for 8 hours or on high for 4 hours, or until a meat thermometer inserted reaches at least 165°F (74°C).
3. Transfer the chicken to a cutting board and pull the meat off the bones, then return the meat to the slow cooker. Shred the meat using two forks, or use a potato masher to speed things up, then stir with the sauce to coat. Serve. (You can also leave the meat on the bone and serve the whole legs if you prefer.)

ALTERNATIVE METHOD

This recipe also works baked in a covered casserole dish in the oven to save time; you'll end up with sticky chicken legs rather than shreddable meat. Bake at 350°F (175°C) for about 1 hour.

WEEKNIGHT CHICKEN DINNER

SERVES 4 TO 6

Remember when your mom got a slow cooker and made every supper in it and it was all mush and tasted the same? No? Just me? My rotisserie chicken seasoning blend makes it super savory, and weekday-friendly as it's mostly hands-off—but you still get that Sunday roast dinner smell running through your house—all without the mush. ;)

ROTISSERIE CHICKEN SEASONING

1 tablespoon paprika

2 teaspoons garlic powder

2 teaspoons onion powder

1 teaspoon poultry seasoning *or* ½ teaspoon dried sage plus ½ teaspoon dried parsley

1 teaspoon salt

¼ teaspoon pepper

CHICKEN & VEGGIES

1 (3-pound/1.5 kg) whole chicken

4 large potatoes (white, red, or yellow), quartered

2 large carrots, peeled and cut into large chunks

1 yellow onion, quartered

¼ cup (60 mL) cold water

2 teaspoons cornstarch

Salt and pepper

1. Grease a slow cooker insert with nonstick cooking spray. Mix together all the seasoning ingredients in a small bowl. Pat the chicken dry with a paper towel and put in the slow cooker, then rub with the seasoning.
2. Add the potatoes, carrots, and onion to the slow cooker. Cover and cook on high for 4 hours or on low for 8 hours, or until a meat thermometer reaches 165°F (74°C). Be sure to check both the thigh and breast.
3. Set the oven to broil. Carefully transfer the chicken and vegetables to a rimmed baking sheet, leaving the juices in the slow cooker. Broil for 3 to 5 minutes, until the chicken skin crisps, watching closely so it doesn't burn.
4. Set the slow cooker back to high. Mix together the water and cornstarch, then whisk the mixture into the juices in the slow cooker. Cook for a few minutes uncovered, stirring constantly, until the gravy thickens. Add a little more cornstarch or water if needed to get the desired consistency. Season the gravy with salt and pepper to taste and serve with the chicken and vegetables.

ALTERNATIVE METHOD

You can also make this in a roasting pan in the oven—the rule of thumb is 15 minutes at 425°F (220°C), then turn down the temperature to 350°F (175°C) and keep roasting for 20 minutes per pound until the internal temperature reaches at least 165°F (74°C). Remember to stir the vegetables once or twice. To make the gravy, either remove the chicken and vegetables from the roasting pan and put the pan directly on the burner, or transfer the liquid to a saucepan.

FARMER CHICKEN & ROASTED POTATOES

SERVES 4 TO 6

CHICKEN

¼ cup (60 mL) soy sauce

¼ cup (60 mL) water

¼ cup (60 mL) neutral oil

2 tablespoons apple cider vinegar

2 tablespoons maple syrup

1 tablespoon Dijon mustard

1 tablespoon Worcestershire sauce

2 teaspoons garlic powder

2 teaspoons onion powder

1 teaspoon dried thyme

¼ teaspoon pepper

2 pounds (1 kg) chicken drumsticks

POTATOES

5 russet potatoes, or any white-fleshed potatoes, scrubbed and cut into 1-inch (2.5 cm) cubes

1 tablespoon olive oil

½ teaspoon salt, plus more to taste

Pepper

WHY: SOAKING THE POTATOES IN COLD WATER REMOVES SOME OF THE STARCH, WHICH ALLOWS THEM TO CRISP UP—THIS IS HOW RESTAURANTS MAKE HAND-CUT FRIES.

WHY: CUTTING INTO MEAT IMMEDIATELY AFTER COOKING LETS OUT ALL THOSE DELICIOUS JUICES.

For years, anytime my son was allowed to pick what we ate for supper, he would proudly request "farmer chicken and potatoes." What about this chicken makes it "farmer"? It's anyone's guess, and mine is that it's made with chicken drumsticks, which are bone-in, and he likened them to chicken "from the farm" (BTW, you can use other cuts of chicken, but you'll need to adjust the cook time accordingly). This marinade is more of a formula than a recipe. The ingredients are flexible, so use what you have! Find more info on making a marinade on page 36. You can make any type of potatoes you like, but I've included a simple roasted potatoes recipe. Pair with corn on the cob for the authentic "farmer chicken" experience.

---

1. To make the marinade, mix together all the ingredients except the chicken in a bowl. Place the chicken in a large zipper-top bag and pour in the marinade. Seal the bag and move the bag around a bit to coat the chicken completely. Refrigerate for at least 1 hour or up to overnight. (Alternatively, you can marinate in a covered casserole dish, but you'll need to turn the chicken occasionally to make sure all sides get marinated.)
2. Soak the potatoes in a bowl of cold water for at least 20 minutes or up to 1 hour, then drain and pat dry.
3. Preheat the oven to 400°F (200°C). Line two rimmed baking sheets with parchment paper. Take the chicken out of the refrigerator and let it rest at room temperature for 10 minutes. Toss the potatoes in the oil, salt, and pepper to taste and spread out in a single layer on one lined baking sheet. **HOT TIP: Make sure the pan is not overcrowded, or the potatoes will not get as crispy.** Bake the potatoes until golden and crispy, about 40 minutes, turning them halfway through.
4. Meanwhile, place the chicken in a single layer on the other lined baking sheet and discard the marinade. Bake until a meat thermometer inserted reaches at least 165°F (74°C), about 35 minutes, then allow the chicken to rest for 5 minutes before serving.

P
S

HYPERFIXATION GREEK CHICKEN SKEWERS & CUCUMBER SALAD

SERVES 4 TO 6

CHICKEN

4 boneless, skinless chicken breasts (about 2 pounds/1 kg), cut into 1-inch (2.5 cm) pieces

½ cup (125 mL) plain Greek yogurt

¼ cup (60 mL) green olive brine

Juice of 1 lemon

2 teaspoons dried oregano

1 teaspoon garlic powder

1 teaspoon onion powder

½ teaspoon salt

¼ teaspoon pepper

SALAD

2 English cucumbers, quartered lengthwise and sliced crosswise

1½ cups grape tomatoes, quartered

¼ medium red onion, finely chopped

1 (6-ounce/200 g) block feta

2 tablespoons Greek yogurt

Juice of ½ lemon

2 tablespoons olive oil

1 teaspoon dried oregano

1 teaspoon dried dill

¼ teaspoon salt

¼ teaspoon pepper

Welcome to the Greek chicken escapades, aka the time I made this every other day for a month with various seasonings. I typically use boneless chicken and make skewers, but this marinade can also be used on pork or bone-in chicken, which are both often more affordable cuts of meat, although cook time will vary. Complete the meal with a Greek salad, and serve warm pita bread alongside, if you like.

1. If using wooden skewers, soak them in warm water for at least 30 minutes to prevent burning. Meanwhile, combine all the chicken ingredients in a large bowl and mix until fully combined and the chicken is coated. Cover and refrigerate for at least 30 minutes, but ideally a few hours or up to overnight.
2. Combine the cucumbers, tomatoes, and onion in a large bowl. Crumble in the feta. In a small bowl, whisk together the yogurt, lemon juice, olive oil, oregano, dill, salt, and pepper. Pour the dressing over the salad and gently stir to coat.
3. Preheat an outdoor grill to medium. Thread the chicken cubes onto 8 skewers. **HOT TIP: I like to wear food-safe latex gloves when doing this as it is messy.** Grill until a meat thermometer inserted reaches 165°F (74°C), 8 to 12 minutes, turning the skewers halfway through. Serve with the salad.

ALTERNATIVE METHOD

The chicken can also be roasted on a rimmed baking sheet in the oven (with or without skewers) at 400°F (200°C) for 10 to 12 minutes, turning halfway through. I've also sautéed them (without skewers) in a large cast-iron skillet—they will release a lot of liquid so you won't get that nice browning, but the flavor is there.

USE WHAT YOU HAVE

OTHER SEASONINGS WE LIKE (USE ABOUT 1 TABLESPOON)	BUT SWAP THE OLIVE JUICE FOR:
Tandoori	Broth, same amount
Jerk	2 tablespoons lime juice or vinegar
Store-bought seasoning mix	Pickle juice, same amount

CORNFLAKE PORK KOTLET & GREEN BEANS

SERVES 4 TO 6

- 2 pounds (1 kg) boneless pork chops
- ⅓ cup (40 g) all-purpose flour
- 2 teaspoons onion powder
- 2 teaspoons garlic powder
- 2 teaspoons salt, plus more to taste
- 1 teaspoon pepper, plus more to taste
- 2 large eggs
- 3 cups cornflakes
- 2 to 4 tablespoons neutral oil
- 2 cups (250 g) trimmed green beans
- ½ cup (50 g) grated Parmesan cheese (optional)

These cornflake pork chops, kotlet schabowy, were a staple when I was living as a nanny in Poland, but I've put my own spin on them. Pork is generally one of the more affordable meats. Loin chops or similar leaner chops are ideal for pounding thin, but you can grab whatever boneless pork cut you like. You'll want to make extra because everyone will want seconds. Pair them with my crispy green beans for a classic supper.

1. Lay the pork chops on a large cutting board and pat dry with paper towels, then cover with a sheet of plastic wrap. Use a flat meat mallet or rolling pin to pound the pork chops down to about ¼ inch (6 mm) thick. **HOT TIP: Getting them thin is important or the breading will burn before the meat is fully cooked.**

2. Prepare the breading station: Mix the flour, onion powder, garlic powder, and salt and pepper in one shallow bowl, beat the eggs in a second shallow bowl, and crush the cornflakes in a third shallow bowl. Working with one pork chop at a time, dredge in the seasoned flour, then in the eggs, then in the cornflakes. **QUICK TIP: Keep one hand dry and one wet to make this easier.**

3. Line a large plate with paper towels. Pour about ¼ inch (6 mm) oil into a large cast-iron or other heavy-bottomed skillet and heat over medium-high heat. Test the oil by dropping in a cornflake from the breading bowl. If the cornflake sizzles immediately, lower a few pork chops into the oil in a single layer, making sure to not crowd the pan. Cook until brown, 2 to 3 minutes per side, then transfer to the prepared plate to drain. Cut one in half to make sure the meat is no longer pink. Repeat until all pork chops are cooked. Let rest for a few minutes before serving.

WHY: CROWDING CAUSES THE OIL TEMPERATURE TO DROP, WHICH WILL RESULT IN GREASY PORK CHOPS.

WHY: SINCE THE CUTLETS ARE VERY THIN, IT'S HARD TO GET AN ACCURATE TEMPERATURE READ WITH A MEAT THERMOMETER.

continues

4. Meanwhile, heat 1 teaspoon oil in a separate large skillet over medium heat. Add the green beans and sauté, stirring occasionally, for about 8 minutes, until the beans are bright green and crisp-tender. Sprinkle with the salt, pepper, and Parmesan (if using), then cover the pan and turn off the heat so the cheese melts. Serve with the pork chops.

USE WHAT YOU HAVE

INGREDIENT	TRY THIS INSTEAD:
Boneless pork chops	Pork loin roast, sliced Boneless, skinless chicken, pounded Thin boneless steak
Cornflakes	Crispy rice cereal
Fresh green beans	Frozen green beans

ALTERNATIVE METHOD

The pork chops can be made in the air fryer, but they will have a baked finish (versus being similar to deep-fried). Air-fry at 400°F (200°C) for 2 minutes, then flip and check every minute or so thereafter as they will cook quickly.

PORK-UPINE & PEPPERS

SERVES 4

ÉPIS

½ yellow bell pepper, roughly chopped

½ green bell pepper, roughly chopped

3 green onions, roughly chopped

2 garlic cloves, roughly chopped

1 celery rib, roughly chopped

1 cup fresh parsley leaves and tender stems

¼ cup neutral oil

Juice of 1 lime

1 tablespoon white vinegar or apple cider vinegar

1 teaspoon vegetable or chicken-flavor bouillon

½ teaspoon ground thyme

¼ teaspoon red pepper flakes, plus more to taste

PORK & VEGETABLES

1 pound (454 g) boneless pork chops or loin, cut into strips

½ medium onion, sliced into thin strips

2 bell peppers, any color, sliced into thin strips

2 teaspoons ground cumin

1 teaspoon garlic powder

1 teaspoon dried thyme

½ teaspoon smoked paprika

½ teaspoon salt

RICE

1½ cups (300 g) white rice

FOR PAN-FRYING

1 tablespoon neutral oil

Don't panic! This isn't a roadkill recipe, it's just pork and peppers. My French brain can't help but go straight to porc-épic (porcupine in French) when I hear "pork épis." If you like chimichurri, you're going to *love* épis. Translated from French, "épis" literally means spice—this sauce is the base for many Haitian dishes. It's made by blending fresh herbs, peppers, and other ingredients. I had the idea to use it to make fajita bowls and swapped in more affordable pork strips. And the result—totally craveable!

1. To make the épis, pulse the bell peppers, green onions, garlic, celery, and parsley in a food processor until finely chopped. Add the oil, lime juice, vinegar, bouillon, thyme, and pepper flakes and pulse until the mixture is somewhat pureed but still has some texture, similar to chimichurri. Measure out ½ cup épis for this recipe; the rest can be stored in the refrigerator for a few days or frozen and used in cooking or meat marinades. **HOT TIP: Use it as a dipping sauce for Garlic Butter Steak Bites (page 64).**
2. Combine the pork, onion, bell peppers, reserved épis, cumin, garlic powder, thyme, smoked paprika, and salt in a large bowl and toss well. Cover and marinate in the refrigerator for at least 1 hour or up to overnight.
3. Cook the rice according to the package directions.
4. Heat the oil in a large cast-iron skillet over medium-high heat. Transfer the pork and vegetables to the pan using tongs, discarding the marinade—be careful, as it will spatter in the hot oil. Cook the pork for a few minutes, until a nice sear develops on one side, then flip using a spatula and repeat until the pork is cooked through and is no longer pink in the center and the vegetables begin to soften, about 8 minutes total, depending the thickness. Serve over the rice.

continues

* This dish is a bit spicy due to the red pepper flakes in the épis. You can make it without them, but that kick really adds something special. If serving to small children, I'd probably set aside some of the meat and vegetables before marinating and cook that separately.

USE WHAT YOU HAVE

INGREDIENT	TRY THIS INSTEAD:
Pork strips	Boneless, skinless chicken Beef
Green bell pepper	2 celery ribs
Orange bell pepper	1 large carrot

BTW . . . The pan needs to be hot so that the liquid from the marinade evaporates, otherwise you won't get a sear. If you notice all the liquid has cooked off before the pork is cooked through, you can turn the heat down a bit to prevent burning.

JUICY SKILLET PORK CHOPS

SERVES 4

1½ cups (300 g) white rice

1 tablespoon neutral oil

4 (¾-inch/2 cm thick) boneless pork chops (about 1½ pounds/680 g)

3 garlic cloves, minced

1 inch (2.5 cm) ginger, minced

¾ cup (185 mL) orange juice

3 tablespoons brown sugar

2 tablespoons soy sauce

1 tablespoon apple cider vinegar

1 tablespoon cornstarch

1 teaspoon toasted sesame oil

¼ teaspoon red pepper flakes (optional)

Pinch ground cinnamon

Sliced green onions, for garnish (optional)

WHY: THIS SAUCE HAS A LOT OF SUGAR, WHICH WILL BURN OVER HIGHER HEAT.

We aren't really a family of juice drinkers, but every so often one of my kids will request orange juice and I end up stuck figuring out what to do with the rest of the carton. Enter orange pork chops, orange chicken, orange tofu . . . you get the picture. Serve over white rice. I like to have steamed frozen broccoli with this dish too.

---

1. Cook the rice according to the package directions.
2. Meanwhile, heat the oil in a large skillet over medium-high heat. Add the pork chops and sear for 1 minute per side. Transfer the pork chops to a plate and turn the heat down to medium. Add the garlic and ginger and sauté, stirring often, for a few minutes to soften.
3. Whisk together the orange juice, brown sugar, soy sauce, vinegar, cornstarch, sesame oil, pepper flakes (if using), and cinnamon in a small bowl.
4. Return the pork chops to the pan, pour the sauce over, and reduce the heat to medium-low. Cook, occasionally spooning the sauce over the pork chops, until a meat thermometer inserted reaches at least 145°F (63°C), about 8 minutes, flipping them halfway through. If the sauce isn't thick enough, you can remove the pork chops and simmer the sauce for another few minutes.
5. Let the pork chops rest for a few minutes before serving (resting helps keep those delicious juices in). Spoon the remaining sauce over the rice and pork chops. Garnish with green onions, if using.

USE WHAT YOU HAVE

INGREDIENT	TRY THIS INSTEAD:
Pork chops	Boneless, skinless chicken Extra-firm tofu, sliced and coated in cornstarch
Pinch ground cinnamon	2 pinches ground allspice

BEST HONEY-GARLIC RIBS

SERVES 4

3 pounds (1.5 kg) pork back ribs

¼ cup (60 g) ghee or melted unsalted butter

5 garlic cloves, minced

1 tablespoon paprika

2 teaspoons onion powder

1 teaspoon salt

½ teaspoon pepper

½ cup (125 mL) honey-garlic sauce

WHY: MEMBRANES ARE EDIBLE BUT THEY CAN MAKE THE RIBS CHEWIER. THEY ALSO KIND OF SEPARATE WHEN YOU'RE CUTTING THE MEAT AND JUST DON'T LOOK APPEALING, SO TRY TO TAKE OFF AS MUCH AS YOU CAN, BUT DON'T SWEAT IT IF YOU CAN'T GET IT ALL.

The idea of cooking ribs always intimidated me, but this recipe is basically two steps, and one of them is in a slow cooker. Make more than you think you need because ribs are half bones, and the meat shrinks when the fat renders off. Alternatively, you can bulk the meal up with more sides to cut costs. I like to soak up all that delicious sauce over mashed potatoes (page 119) and pair with cheesy cauliflower (page 206).

1. Place the ribs on a large cutting board, meaty side down, and use a paper towel to grip a corner of the membrane and pull to remove. **HOT TIP: Sometimes you need to use a butter knife to separate a corner from the meat so you can grip it.** Pat the ribs dry and cut into 3-to-5-rib pieces that will fit in the slow cooker.
2. In a small bowl, combine the ghee, garlic, paprika, onion powder, salt, and pepper and mix well. Layer the ribs in the slow cooker, painting them lightly with the garlic mixture. Cover and cook on high for 4 hours or on low for up to 8 hours.
3. Set the oven to broil. Line a rimmed baking sheet with aluminum foil and lay the cooked ribs out in a single layer, meaty side up. Paint the ribs with the honey-garlic sauce and broil for 3 to 5 minutes to caramelize the sauce, watching closely so the ribs don't burn. Serve.

BTW . . . SIDE RIBS TEND TO GO ON SALE MORE OFTEN THAN BACK RIBS, AND YOU CAN TOTALLY USE THOSE HERE. I DO FIND THEY HAVE LESS MEAT ON THEM AND THE MEMBRANE IS HARDER TO PULL OFF. SOMETIMES YOU GET WHAT YOU PAY FOR.

SLOW COOKER SMOKED SAUSAGE & POTATOES

SERVES 4 TO 6

1½ pounds (750 g) baby red or yellow potatoes

2 medium carrots, peeled and roughly chopped

1 medium yellow onion, roughly chopped

1 tablespoon neutral oil

2 teaspoons garlic powder

1 teaspoon paprika

1 teaspoon dried oregano

½ teaspoon salt

¼ teaspoon pepper

1 pound (454 g) smoked sausage links

As a time saver on my kids' sports nights, I love to prep supper while I'm making lunch. Dump-and-go meals like this smoked sausage and potato dinner are perfect to throw in the slow cooker, and everything's done by the time we get home. You can play around with the ingredients and seasonings based on what you have on hand. The trick is to not add any liquid, since the veggies will release a bit anyway.

1. Combine the potatoes, carrots, onion, oil, garlic powder, paprika, oregano, salt, and pepper in a slow cooker and stir to coat. Lay the sausages over the vegetables. Cover and cook on high for 4 hours or on low for 8 hours. If can, give everything a stir halfway through so the potatoes get some crisp on more than one spot, but this is not a critical step. Serve.

TRY THESE COMBINATIONS

SAUSAGE	VEGETABLE	SWAP DRIED OREGANO FOR:
Cheddar, smoked	Broccoli (add in final hour)	Dried parsley
Honey-garlic, fresh	Sweet potato	Dried rosemary
Italian, fresh	Sliced zucchini, grape tomatoes (add in final hour)	Italian seasoning

WHITE FISH IN THE PAN

SERVES 4 TO 6

⅔ cup (80 g) all-purpose flour
2 teaspoons paprika
2 teaspoons garlic powder
2 teaspoons onion powder
2 teaspoons dried parsley
1 teaspoon dried dill
1 teaspoon salt
½ teaspoon pepper
2 tablespoons butter, divided
2 tablespoons neutral oil, divided
6 white fish fillets (2 to 3 pounds/1 to 1.5 kg)

WHY: BUTTER FOR FLAVOR; OIL SO IT DOESN'T BURN.

It's always a special treat when we have white fish for supper. Despite Nova Scotia having a strong fishing industry, fresh fish isn't always affordable. I typically use frozen (thawed) fillets as I've found them to be the best bang for my buck (especially if I catch a sale), but you can use either. I serve this with simple roasted potatoes and my broccoli covered in Cheese Sauce Makes Everything Better (page 206)—so this whole meal comes together in under 20 minutes.

1. Mix together the flour, paprika, garlic powder, onion powder, parsley, dill, salt, and pepper in a shallow bowl.
2. Heat 1 tablespoon each butter and oil in a large nonstick skillet over medium heat.
3. Dredge 3 fish fillets, one at a time, in the flour mixture to coat, then gently lower into the pan. Cook undisturbed for 5 minutes, then gently flip and cook for another 3 minutes, or until a meat thermometer inserted reaches at least 145°F (63°C) and the fish flakes easily with a fork. **HOT TIP: Fish fillets are thin and your thermometer is going to hit the hot pan, so you'll need to gently lift the fillet out of the pan with a spatula and insert the thermometer at an angle to get an accurate temperature reading.**
4. Repeat with the remaining 1 tablespoon each butter and oil to cook the remaining 3 fillets. Serve.

BTW . . . I USUALLY LOSE SOME OF THE COATING STUCK TO THE PAN WHEN FLIPPING. IT'S WORTH SCRAPING OFF AND PLATING WITH THE FISH—YUM!

SHEET PAN DINNER TABLE

The whole point of sheet pan dinners is to make a great meal when you don't feel like cooking (at least that's when I make them!). Bonus: They are a great way to clean out your refrigerator. The options are literally endless. Here are my hot tips for fool-proofing your next sheet pan dinner.

BTW . . . SEASONING SHOULD BE ADDED BEFORE COOKING. SOME SAUCES ARE INTENDED TO USE FOR DIPPING OR TO BE EATEN COLD (SALSA, SOUR CREAM), SO LEAVE THOSE OFF UNTIL SERVING. SAUCES THAT HAVE A HIGH SUGAR CONTENT (BBQ, TERIYAKI) SHOULD BE ADDED NEAR THE END OF COOKING TO AVOID BURNING (SUGAR TENDS TO BURN WHEN COOKED TOO LONG).

1. Preheat the oven to 400°F (200°C)—most food will cook well at this temp. Expect it to take 20 to 40 minutes, turning once. Use a meat thermometer to check the meat and pierce the veggies with a fork to check doneness.
2. Don't cut all the veggies the same size—cut them according to cook time. A good rule of thumb is to cut harder vegetables like carrots smaller and leave softer vegetables like zucchini bigger.
3. When in doubt, separate it out: Put the meat on a separate sheet pan, or on one part of the pan, instead of mixing everything together. This way you can take one component out of the oven if it's done cooking ahead of the rest.
4. Use the same mixing bowl, seasoning one component after the other, or oil and season directly on the sheet pan to save time and one more bowl to wash.
5. Get creative! There are no wrong answers. Here are some combinations we like:

DINNER	PROTEIN	VEGETABLES	STARCH	SAUCE & SEASONING*
SAUSAGE & PEPPERS	Sausages	Bell peppers, onions	Serve on sausage buns	Dried basil. Top buns with cooked sausage and peppers, then marinara and cheese, and return to oven briefly to melt.
TERIYAKI SALMON	Salmon	Broccoli, asparagus	Sweet potatoes	Teriyaki sauce
GNOCCHI	Chickpeas	Green beans	Gnocchi	Nutritional yeast, garlic powder
CHICKEN	Chicken drumsticks	Corn on the cob	Potatoes	Seasoning blend of choice
FAUX-MEATLOAF	Meatballs	Carrots, onions	Potatoes	Ketchup
QUESADILLAS	Cheese, black beans	Tomato, onion, bell pepper	Tortillas	Salsa, sour cream
PINEAPPLE PORK	Pork chops	Bell pepper, onion, pineapple	Sweet potatoes	BBQ sauce

GARLIC BUTTER STEAK BITES

SERVES 4 TO 6

2 pounds (1 kg) sirloin tip roast or flank steak (look for some marbling), sliced against the grain into ½-inch (1 cm) thick pieces (For a more detailed how-to, see page 36.)

3 tablespoons neutral oil, divided

2 teaspoons white vinegar

1 tablespoon Worcestershire sauce

3 garlic cloves, minced

½ teaspoon salt, plus more to taste

½ teaspoon pepper, plus more to taste

½ teaspoon baking soda

¼ cup (60 g) butter

BTW . . . DURING THE PHOTO SHOOT FOR THE BOOK, WE WANTED TO ADD SOME COLOR TO THE PICTURE, SO WE ADDED A DIPPING SAUCE—THE BRIGHT GREEN "ÉPIS" FROM PORK-UPINE & PEPPERS (PAGE 55). IT TURNED OUT TO BE SO GOOD—TRY IT!

Steak is definitely a luxury these days, but you can make a cheap cut of meat tender without having to slow cook it. TikTok taught me about velveting, a method often found in Chinese cooking that uses baking soda to tenderize the meat. It works best when the beef is cut into small pieces so the baking soda can work its magic all over.

1. Combine the beef strips, 2 tablespoons of the oil, the vinegar, Worcestershire, garlic, salt, and pepper in a large bowl and toss to coat. Sprinkle the baking soda over the beef a little at a time, mixing to coat. Let sit for about 30 minutes, then pat the beef dry with a paper towel.
2. Heat the remaining 1 tablespoon oil along with the butter in a cast-iron or other heavy-bottomed skillet over medium-high heat. Add the beef and cook undisturbed for about 2 minutes, so a sear forms.
3. Flip the beef pieces, season with salt and pepper to taste, and spoon the melted butter over the top. **HOT TIP: I find the easiest way to do this is to tip the pan slightly, holding the handle with an oven mitt if using cast iron, and scoop the melted butter that pools near the tilted edge.** Cook for another 2 minutes, then flip any pieces that still have unseared sides, transferring those that look cooked to a plate and let rest a few minutes.

USE WHAT YOU HAVE

INGREDIENT	TRY THIS INSTEAD:
Beef	Boneless pork loin (not tenderloin—you want the "whiter"-looking pork meat)
White vinegar	Apple cider vinegar
Baking soda	1 teaspoon baking powder

SALISBURY STEAKS

SERVES 6

1 pound (454 g) ground beef

8 saltine crackers, crushed

1 medium onion, finely chopped, divided

1 large egg

2 teaspoons prepared mustard

1 teaspoon garlic powder

¼ teaspoon salt

¼ teaspoon pepper

1 tablespoon neutral oil

2 tablespoons butter

2 tablespoons all-purpose flour

2 teaspoons beef bouillon

2 teaspoons Worcestershire sauce

1 cup (250 mL) water, or more as needed

Every time I make a meal that's inspired by a frozen dinner, but from scratch, my kids gobble it up. Salisbury steak is much more affordable than grilled steak, plus what kid doesn't love a hamburger? Serve with mashed potatoes and kid-approved veggies such as boiled carrots and corn.

1. In a large bowl, combine the beef, crushed saltines, one-third of the onion, egg, mustard, garlic powder, salt, and pepper. Mix with a fork to combine thoroughly. **HOT TIP: Let the mixture sit for 5 minutes for the saltines to soften; it will help the patties bind better.** Divide and form the meat mixture into 6 equal patties flattened to about ½ inch (1 cm) thick.
2. Heat the oil in a large skillet over medium heat. Gently place the patties in the pan and sear for 3 minutes, then flip and cook for 3 minutes on the other side. Transfer to a plate.
3. Add the butter and remaining onion to the pan and sauté, stirring occasionally, until the onion is soft and translucent, about 5 minutes. Mix in the flour and cook for 1 minute. Whisk in the beef bouillon, Worcestershire sauce, and water until the mixture is smooth and begins to thicken. Add more water as needed to create the desired gravy consistency.
4. Reduce the heat to low and return the beef patties to the pan. Spoon some of the gravy over them, cover, and cook for 5 minutes to allow the flavors to meld before serving.

USE WHAT YOU HAVE

INGREDIENT	TRY THIS INSTEAD:
Ground beef	Ground pork
Saltines	Bread crumbs, oats
Worcestershire sauce	1 teaspoon soy sauce + 1 teaspoon sugar
Gravy ingredients	Condensed mushroom soup (skip step 3)

SNEAKY TURKEY MEATBALLS

SERVES 6 TO 8

1 (19-ounce/540 mL) can brown lentils, rinsed and drained, *or* 2 cups (400 g) cooked brown lentils

1 large egg

1 pound (454 g) ground turkey or any ground meat

2 cups (200 g) shredded mozzarella cheese (optional)

½ cup rolled oats

1 teaspoon Worcestershire sauce (optional)

2 teaspoons garlic powder

2 teaspoons onion powder

2 teaspoons Italian seasoning

½ teaspoon salt

¼ teaspoon pepper

These turkey meatballs go out to all the wannabe lentil haters, aka my kids and their friends. Trust me when I say this is a don't-ask-don't-tell kinda situation. I love mixing beans or lentils in with meat to stretch the portion as a budget hack. Plus, most of us could use a bit more fiber anyway. Add these meatballs to my Hidden Veggie Pasta Primavera (page 95), or serve them on their own with ketchup for dipping. I like to freeze half after cooking for a future meal, which I usually reheat in the air fryer from frozen.

---

1. Preheat the oven to 400°F (200°C). Line a rimmed baking sheet with parchment paper.
2. In a food processor or blender, combine the lentils and egg and pulse until loosely pureed. If you have neither appliance, try to mash the lentils a bit with a fork.
3. Transfer the mixture to a large bowl and add the turkey, mozzarella (if using), oats, Worcestershire (if using), garlic powder, onion powder, Italian seasoning, salt, and pepper. Mix until well incorporated, using your hands if needed. Allow the mixture to sit for 5 minutes.
4. Roll the mixture into balls about 1 inch (2.5 cm) in diameter and place on the lined baking sheet. **QUICK TIP: Use a small cookie scoop to form the meatballs faster.** Bake until a meat thermometer inserted reaches at least 165°F (74°C), 10 to 12 minutes. Serve.

WHY: MASHING THE LENTILS WILL HELP THE MEATBALLS HOLD TOGETHER BETTER.

WHY: THIS WILL ALLOW THE OATS TO SOAK UP THE LIQUID AND HELP BIND THE MEATBALLS.

USE WHAT YOU HAVE

SUB OATS WITH:
½ cup breadcrumbs or panko
½ cup crushed crackers
1 bread heel, toasted and torn into tiny pieces
1 packet boxed stuffing mix (dry) plus half the seasoning called for

BTW . . . I LIKE ADDING CHEESE FOR THE FLAVOR, BUT YOU DON'T NEED TO CHANGE THE RECIPE IN ANY WAY IF YOU WANT TO OMIT IT.

FAKEOUT SWEET & SOUR TOFU

SERVES 2 TO 4

- 1 cup (200 g) rice of choice, or more if desired
- 1 pound (454 g) extra-firm tofu, frozen and thawed if desired, drained
- ¼ cup (28 g) cornstarch
- 2 large eggs
- 2 to 4 tablespoons neutral oil
- ⅔ cup (140 g) packed brown sugar, or more if you like it sweet
- ⅓ cup (75 mL) ketchup
- ⅓ cup (75 mL) seasoned rice vinegar
- 2 tablespoons low-sodium soy sauce
- 2 teaspoons toasted sesame oil
- 1 teaspoon garlic powder
- 1 teaspoon onion powder
- ½ teaspoon ground ginger

This sweet-and-sour tofu recipe is my best hack for satisfying that takeout craving when my wallet says we have takeout at home. If you're cooking for a group, I recommend doubling (or even tripling) the recipe. I know I say We Use What We Have and that's true, but if you're using tofu, it has to be extra-firm for this recipe, as anything softer won't hold up texture-wise. I usually serve this over plain basmati rice or whip up a quick fried rice. If I'm feeling extra, I'll also grab a pack of vegetable egg rolls from the freezer section as a side.

1. Cook the rice according to the package directions.
2. Meanwhile, rip the tofu into largish chunks and squeeze the water out by hand. **HOT TIP: If you've made tofu in the past with bad results and you skipped this step—this is where you went wrong—nobody wants to eat a soggy sponge.** Put the tofu in a large bowl. Pour the cornstarch over the tofu and stir to coat. Crack the eggs in and stir to coat—no need to individually bread the pieces.
3. Heat about ¼ inch (6 mm) oil in a large skillet over medium heat. Drop one piece of tofu in as a test. If it sizzles, the oil is hot enough. If the oil isn't hot enough, the tofu will absorb more oil and the dish will be greasy. Pour the remaining tofu into the pan in a single layer and use a spatula to separate the pieces. Once the bottoms start to brown, stir the pieces and continue cooking until they are golden on all sides, 10 to 15 minutes total.
4. Meanwhile, mix together the brown sugar, ketchup, vinegar, soy sauce, sesame oil, garlic powder, onion powder, and ginger in a small bowl. Turn the heat down to medium-low. If oil remains in the pan, drain it, then pour the sauce over the tofu, stirring to coat. Continue cooking, stirring occasionally, until the sauce thickens, about 15 minutes. Serve over the rice.

ALTERNATIVE METHOD

If you don't have a pan large enough to fit everything in step 4, transfer the tofu to a glass baking dish that has been coated with nonstick cooking spray, pour the sauce over, and bake at 375°F (190°C) for about 20 minutes, stirring halfway through.

USE WHAT YOU HAVE

INGREDIENT	TRY THIS INSTEAD:
Tofu	Boneless, skinless chicken or pork
Eggs	3 tablespoons ground flax + 9 tablespoons milk; let thicken for 5 minutes
Seasoned rice vinegar	Apple cider vinegar

CHAPTER TWO

PASTA & NOODLES

Pasta and noodles never let me down. They're quick, easy, and affordable, and I know my kids will eat them. I love cleaning out my fridge and throwing pasta together with a bunch of leftovers or odds and ends (see Happy Cheeseburger Macaroni, page 85), but I also love a thought-out meal (like my Grown-Up Butter Noodles & Chicken Nuggets, page 74—you have to try it!). In this chapter you'll find a mix of those as well as some stir-fry noodle-style recipes.

GROWN-UP BUTTER NOODLES & CHICKEN NUGGETS

SERVES 6 TO 8

My kids would eat butter noodles and chicken nuggets any day, but it's not for me, so I set out to make a version that appeals to me and other adults but is still very kid-friendly. The result is an easy and worthwhile recipe to make when you have boneless, skinless chicken breasts on hand. Bonus: You can get this meal on the table in under 30 minutes. Round it out with a quick vegetable side like steamed broccoli.

2 pounds (1 kg) boneless, skinless chicken breasts, patted dry and cut into 1-inch (2.5 cm) pieces

⅓ cup (40 g) all-purpose flour

2 teaspoons baking powder

1 tablespoon dried parsley

1 teaspoon garlic powder

1 teaspoon onion powder

1 teaspoon salt

½ teaspoon pepper

¼ cup (60 g) butter, divided

2 tablespoons olive oil, divided

3 or 4 garlic cloves

1 (1-pound/454 g) package pappardelle or other long noodles

1 cup reserved pasta water

1½ cups (150 g) grated Parmesan or other hard cheese

BTW . . . I DON'T BELIEVE IN BREADING LITTLE PIECES INDIVIDUALLY—IT'S NOT NECESSARY UNLESS YOU ARE DOING MULTISTEP BREADING (FOR EXAMPLE, FLOUR, EGG, BREADCRUMBS), AND IF I HAD TO DO IT THAT WAY I WOULDN'T BREAD THINGS AT ALL

1. Put the chicken a large bowl. Mix together the flour, baking powder, parsley, garlic powder, onion powder, salt, and pepper in a small bowl. Sprinkle over the chicken and toss to coat.
2. Melt 2 tablespoons of the butter along with 1 tablespoon of the oil in a heavy-bottomed skillet over medium heat. Add the chicken in a single layer, then press the garlic directly over the chicken with a garlic press (or mince it separately, but the name of the game for me is easy). Cook, occasionally flipping the chicken pieces, until a meat thermometer inserted reaches 165°F (74°C), 7 to 10 minutes depending how crowded your pan is. Add the remaining 2 tablespoons butter and remaining 1 tablespoon oil and gently toss the chicken to coat as the butter melts. Transfer the chicken to a plate.
3. While the chicken is cooking, bring a large pot of lightly salted water to a boil and cook the pasta to al dente according to the package directions. Reserve 1 cup (250 mL) of the pasta water, then drain the pasta.
4. Add the pasta to the pan and sprinkle with the Parmesan, tossing to coat the pasta in the butter and garlic remaining in the pan. Add the reserved pasta water a little at a time until the Parmesan forms a saucy coating on the pasta (you may not need all of it). Return the chicken to the pan, stir it all together, and serve.

UNCLE KEVIN'S PORK RAGOUT

SERVES 4 TO 6

- 1 tablespoon neutral oil
- 1 pound (454 g) Italian sausages, removed from casings
- 2 celery ribs, finely chopped
- 1 carrot, peeled and finely chopped
- ½ red bell pepper, finely chopped
- ½ medium onion, finely chopped
- 2 garlic cloves, minced
- 1 teaspoon dried basil
- 1 teaspoon dried thyme
- 1 teaspoon garlic powder
- 1 teaspoon onion powder
- 1 (24-ounce or 680 mL) can or jar tomato sauce
- 1 teaspoon balsamic vinegar
- 2 teaspoons sugar
- ¼ teaspoon pepper
- Salt
- 1 (12-ounce/340 g) package jumbo shells or pasta of choice
- Grated Parmesan cheese, for topping (optional)

BTW . . . I'M CONVINCED ALL CANNED TOMATO VARIETIES ARE CLOSE ENOUGH AND YOU CAN USE WHAT YOU HAVE: WATER DOWN TOMATO PASTE; CRUSHED TOMATOES ARE A BIT WATERIER BUT WORK IN A PINCH; PASTA SAUCE IS JUST TOMATO SAUCE WITH MORE FLAVOR.

My mother-in-law will proudly tell you she doesn't like sausage, but you know what she does like? Uncle Kevin's (her son's) pork ragout, a tomato-based pasta sauce that's slow simmered . . . using pork sausage that was removed from the casings! Anyway, that's our little secret. ;)

1. Heat the oil in an electric pressure cooker or large skillet over medium heat. Add the sausage meat and sauté, stirring often, until it begins to brown, about 5 minutes. Add the celery, carrot, bell pepper, onion, and garlic and cook until the vegetables soften and the meat is cooked through, another 5 minutes. Add the tomato sauce, vinegar, sugar, and pepper. If using a pressure cooker, set to pressure cook on high for 20 minutes, then natural release. If cooking on the stovetop, bring to a simmer and cook for 40 minutes. If the sauce begins to spatter, reduce the heat slightly.
2. Meanwhile, bring a large pot of lightly salted water to a boil and cook the pasta shells to al dente according to the package directions. Reserve ¼ cup (60 mL) of the pasta water, then drain the pasta. Return the pasta to the pot.
3. Add the reserved pasta water and ¼ cup of the pasta sauce to the cooked pasta and mix well—a little trick to help the sauce stick better and keep the pasta from sticking together. Serve the pasta with a generous scoop of sauce so it gets into the shells. Top with Parmesan, if using.

USE WHAT YOU HAVE

INGREDIENT	TRY THIS INSTEAD:
Italian sausage	Ground pork or ground chicken + 1 teaspoon Italian seasoning
1 teaspoon balsamic vinegar + 2 teaspoons sugar	2 teaspoons balsamic glaze OR 2 tablespoons red wine + 1 teaspoon sugar
Celery, carrot, or bell pepper	More of another vegetable, or add zucchini or mushrooms

CREAMY CABBAGE & KIELBASA SKILLET

SERVES 4

1 tablespoon neutral oil

2 tablespoons butter, divided

1 medium onion, finely chopped

3 garlic cloves, minced

8 ounces (250 g) kielbasa*, quartered lengthwise and sliced ¼-inch (6 mm) thick crosswise

½ small cabbage, sliced into pieces about the size of the egg noodles

2 teaspoons dried oregano

¼ teaspoon pepper, plus more to taste

2 tablespoons chicken bouillon

2 teaspoons Dijon mustard

1 (12-ounce/340 g) package extra-broad egg noodles

4 cups (950 mL) water

1 cup (250 mL) half-and-half or 10% cream

Salt

Cabbage is one of my daughter's favorite veggies—she will even munch on it raw. And while her siblings aren't quite as enthusiastic, I'm also convinced they don't taste it much in this recipe. So between us, there are definitely *no* vegetables in this recipe—only green noodles. It's basically macaroni and hot dogs . . . and a whole lot of "mommy marketing." ;)

1. Heat the oil in a large nonstick skillet over medium heat. Add 1 tablespoon of the butter, the onion, garlic, and kielbasa and sauté, stirring often, until the onion is translucent and the kielbasa begins to brown, about 5 minutes.
2. Mix in the cabbage, oregano, and pepper and cook until soft. The cook time will depend on how soft you want the cabbage. I personally enjoy a little crunch, which takes about 10 minutes, but if you're trying to hide the cabbage, you'll want to cook it for about 20 minutes. Be sure to stir occasionally to avoid burning on the bottom.
3. Add the bouillon, Dijon, uncooked egg noodles, and water and mix to combine, then bring to a low boil and cook until the noodles are al dente, about 7 minutes. Pour in the half-and-half and continue cooking for a few minutes, until the sauce thickens. Taste and add salt and pepper if desired, then serve.

*INSPECT YOUR KIELBASA FOR A REMOVABLE CASING BEFORE SLICING. SOME BRANDS HAVE A FILM THAT NEEDS TO BE REMOVED BEFORE COOKING. IT CAN LOOK LIKE AN EDIBLE CASING BUT PEELS OFF EASILY.

USE WHAT YOU HAVE

INGREDIENT	TRY THIS INSTEAD:
Kielbasa	Bacon (omit cooking oil)
Dijon mustard	2 tablespoons white wine OR 1 teaspoon white wine vinegar + 1 teaspoon yellow mustard (but it will be yellow)
Chicken bouillon	Vegetable bouillon OR 1 tablespoon nutritional yeast + 1 teaspoon salt + 1 teaspoon garlic powder + 1 teaspoon onion powder + 1 teaspoon dried parsley + ½ teaspoon dried oregano + ½ teaspoon dried thyme
Egg noodles	Macaroni or rotini (look for smaller pasta without ridges)

WHOLE EGG CARBONARA

SERVES 4 TO 6

1 (18-ounce/500 g) package bacon

1 (1 pound/454 g) box linguine or other long pasta

2 cups (300 g) frozen petite peas

1 cup (250 mL) reserved pasta water

5 large eggs

3 cups (300 g) grated Parmesan or other similar hard cheese

1½ teaspoons garlic powder

½ teaspoon pepper

You know what bugs me? Recipes that call for only egg yolks or egg whites. In this economy I'm not wasting multiple half eggs, and honestly I don't think you need to, so I created this carbonara pasta that uses bacon fat to make up the difference. Carbonara can seem intimidating, but it's pretty much foolproof and also picky-eater-proof—my kids will even eat the leftovers.

1. Preheat the oven to 400°F (200°C). Line a rimmed baking sheet with parchment paper.
2. Lay out the bacon strips in a single layer on the lined baking sheet and bake for 15 minutes, then flip them and bake for another 5 minutes, or until the bacon is crispy but not burnt. **HOT TIP: Keep a close eye on the bacon, as each brand seems cut to different thicknesses, so cook time may vary.** Transfer the bacon to a paper towel–lined plate to drain. Reserve 2 tablespoons of the bacon grease for the pasta.
3. Meanwhile, bring a pot of lightly salted water to a boil. **HOT TIP: Be careful not to oversalt as there are many other salty components in the dish—you can always add more later, but you can't take it out.** Cook the pasta to al dente according to the package directions, adding the frozen peas in the last few minutes. Reserve 1 cup (250 mL) of the pasta water, then drain the pasta and peas and return them to the pot.
4. Whisk together the eggs, Parmesan, garlic powder, and pepper in a bowl. Stir the reserved bacon grease into the drained pasta to coat, then pour in the egg mixture and mix vigorously.
5. Mix in ½ cup (125 mL) of the reserved pasta water and stir. Return to low heat and continue stirring constantly with a silicone spatula until the sauce thickens and coats the pasta, 1 to 2 minutes. If needed, stir in more pasta water, ¼ cup (60 mL) at a time, to form a glossy sauce. Using a silicone spatula lets you swipe along the bottom of the pan to see how things are cooking and determine if more liquid is needed. Crumble the cooked bacon into the pasta and serve.

WHY: LOWERING THE HEAT AND MIXING CONSTANTLY ARE IMPORTANT, OTHERWISE YOU MAY END UP WITH SCRAMBLED EGGS INSTEAD OF A SMOOTH SAUCE.

WEEKNIGHT BEEF STROGANOFF

SERVES 6

1 pound (454 g) beef stew meat cubes

½ teaspoon salt, plus more to taste

¼ teaspoon pepper, plus more to taste

8 ounces (227 g) cremini or white mushrooms, sliced

½ medium onion, sliced

3 garlic cloves, minced

1 tablespoon butter

2 teaspoons Worcestershire sauce

1 teaspoon balsamic vinegar

1 teaspoon dried thyme

1 (10-ounce/284 mL) can condensed cream of mushroom soup

2¼ cups (560 mL) beef broth

1 (12-ounce/340 g) package broad egg noodles

⅓ cup (85 mL) plain Greek yogurt

Calling all mushroom lovers who live with not-so-mushroom-lovers! This is the recipe I used to convert my husband many years ago, and now I put them in everything. The beef is brown, the mushrooms are brown—you can barely tell they're in there. Plus, it's a great way to stretch meat without losing those rich flavors and textures.

I chose beef stew meat for this recipe because it is typically more affordable, but we thin slice it, so the cut really doesn't matter—if your store has another cut for a better price, get that instead!

1. Grease a slow cooker insert with nonstick cooking spray. Trim the beef of any tough membranes and overly thick fat, then slice it thin and season with the salt and pepper. Add it to the slow cooker, along with the mushrooms, onion, garlic, butter, Worcestershire sauce, vinegar, thyme, mushroom soup, and beef broth (I fill the can twice). Cover and cook on low for 8 hours or on high for 3 to 4 hours, until the beef and mushrooms are tender.
2. Set the slow cooker to high if not already and mix in the egg noodles. Cover and cook for 10 minutes, then stir and cook for another 5 to 10 minutes. The time will depend on how hot your slow cooker runs. Stir in the yogurt and season with additional salt and pepper if desired. Serve.

ALTERNATIVE METHOD

This recipe can be made as a one-pan stovetop meal. Sauté the onion, mushrooms, and beef in 1 tablespoon neutral oil in a Dutch oven over medium heat until the beef is browned and the mushrooms soften. Add the garlic and cook a few more minutes, then mix in all the remaining ingredients except the yogurt. Cover and simmer until the noodles are cooked, stirring occasionally. If the liquid is absorbed before the noodles are done, add water, ¼ cup (60 mL) at a time. Mix in the yogurt and serve.

USE WHAT YOU HAVE

INGREDIENT	TRY THIS INSTEAD:	NOTES
Beef strips	Ground beef	Sauté the beef on the stovetop—slow cooker not necessary
Beef broth	Bouillon + water	
Egg noodles	Pasta	Cook time will be a bit longer
Greek yogurt	Sour cream	
Balsamic vinegar and Worcestershire sauce	Can omit	

HAPPY CHEESEBURGER MACARONI

SERVES 4

1 pound (454 g) ground beef

1 small onion, finely chopped

2 garlic cloves, minced

1½ cups (225 g) fresh green beans, sliced on the bias, or frozen French-cut green beans

1 teaspoon garlic powder

½ teaspoon pepper

¼ teaspoon salt, plus more to taste

1 (7.25-ounce/200 g) box macaroni and cheese

2 cups (500 mL) water

1 cup (100 g) shredded cheddar cheese

1 tablespoon ketchup

2 teaspoons yellow mustard

2 teaspoons relish

¼ cup crispy fried onions (optional)

WHY: ONIONS SWEAT, SO YOU WANT TO DRAIN THE GREASE BEFORE ADDING THEM TO AVOID POURING OUT ANY OF THAT DELICIOUS ONION JUICE.

When I was a university student, I was shopping for one on a budget so I couldn't always get every ingredient to cook from scratch. This one-pot cheeseburger macaroni was a weekly staple. Whether you need to save time, budget, or cupboard space, doctoring up packaged foods is a great way to elevate them while also developing your We Use What We Have cooking skills. Add whatever veggies you need to use up—it doesn't matter if you wouldn't put them on an actual cheeseburger, as somehow it still works.

1. Sauté the ground beef in a large nonstick skillet over medium heat until it begins to brown, about 7 minutes. Drain off any fat, then add the onion and sauté until translucent, about 5 minutes.
2. Add the garlic powder, pepper, and salt and mix well, then add the macaroni (but not the cheese powder yet) and water. Cook, stirring occasionally, until the pasta is al dente and the water has been absorbed, about 8 minutes. If the water evaporates before the pasta is done, you can add a bit more.
3. Add the cheese powder (no need for butter or milk here), mix to combine, then stir in the cheddar cheese, ketchup, mustard, and relish. Sprinkle each bowl with a tablespoon of crispy fried onions, if using. Serve.

USE WHAT YOU HAVE

This is really an "anything goes" recipe—use what you have! Here are some other combinations I like that use up leftover meat:

PROTEIN	VEGGIE
Rotisserie chicken	Broccoli or cauliflower
Pulled pork	Bell pepper + onion
Sausages	Zucchini or corn

ZESTY LEMON TUNA PASTA

SERVES 3

10 ounces/300 g spaghettini*

1 head broccoli, cut into small florets, *or* 3 cups (300 g) frozen broccoli florets

½ cup (125 mL) olive oil, divided

2 (6-ounce/170 g) cans tuna, drained

4 garlic cloves, minced

¼ teaspoon red pepper flakes (optional)

Grated zest and juice of 1 large lemon

3 tablespoons nutritional yeast

2 teaspoons dried parsley *or* 2 tablespoons chopped fresh parsley

1 teaspoon dried oregano

1 teaspoon salt

¼ teaspoon pepper

Lemon tuna pasta became a weekly staple as I transitioned back to meat-eating after two years as a vegan (more on that on page 12). It's a comfort meal that's also fresh and super affordable, with mostly pantry staples. Nutritional yeast is an ingredient used in a lot of vegan recipes to replace cheese flavor. You can usually find it in the natural foods section of the grocery store, but I've included swaps, and you can also leave it out (but the recipe will have less flavor).

1. Bring a pot of lightly salted water to a boil and cook the spaghettini to al dente according to the package directions, adding the broccoli when 3 minutes remain. Drain and return the pasta and broccoli to the pot.
2. Heat ¼ cup (60 mL) of the oil in a large nonstick skillet over medium heat. Add the tuna, garlic, and red pepper flakes (if using) and sauté until the garlic softens and the tuna begins to get some crispy bits, about 5 minutes. Reduce the heat to medium-low if the garlic is browning too quickly. Add the tuna mixture to the pasta in the pot.
3. In a small bowl, mix together the lemon zest and juice, the remaining ¼ cup (60 mL) oil, nutritional yeast, parsley, oregano, salt, and pepper. Add to the pasta in the pot and mix to coat. Serve.

USE WHAT YOU HAVE

INGREDIENT	TRY THIS INSTEAD:
Spaghettini	Spaghetti or fettuccine
Broccoli	Kale
Canned tuna	Leftover rotisserie chicken
Olive oil	Canola oil, but the flavor will be more neutral
Nutritional yeast	Grated Parmesan, but reduce the salt

* IF YOU'RE WORKING WITH A 1-POUND (454 G) PACKAGE OF PASTA, USE ABOUT TWO-THIRDS OF IT. NO NEED TO WEIGH IT, CLOSE IS GOOD ENOUGH!

NO-BOIL TUNA LASAGNA CASSEROLE

SERVES 4

2 (6-ounce/170 g) cans tuna, drained

1 carrot, peeled and shredded

½ cup (75 g) frozen peas

1½ cups (150 g) shredded mozzarella cheese

1½ cups (150 g) shredded cheddar cheese

1 (10-ounce/284 mL) can condensed cream of mushroom soup

½ cup (125 mL) milk

½ cup (125 mL) water

1 teaspoon chicken bouillon

1 teaspoon garlic powder

1 teaspoon onion powder

½ teaspoon dried oregano

¼ teaspoon pepper

⅛ teaspoon salt

6 traditional (not no-boil!) lasagna noodles

If you like tuna casserole, you will *love* this tuna lasagna. It's so easy to prepare, my eight-year-old can do it on her own. This recipe uses regular lasagna noodles, but you don't have to boil them because I've accounted for that in the liquid and cook time. I like to serve this with a simple salad for a family-friendly dinner.

1. Preheat the oven to 375°F (190°C). Grease an 8 × 8-inch casserole dish with nonstick cooking spray.
2. In a large bowl, mix together the tuna, carrot, peas, 1 cup (100 g) of the mozzarella, 1 cup (100 g) of the cheddar, the cream of mushroom soup, milk, water, bouillon, garlic powder, onion powder, oregano, pepper, and salt.
3. Spread a thin layer of the tuna mixture in the bottom of the casserole dish, then a single layer of the uncooked lasagna noodles, breaking some if needed to make them fit. Spoon another, more generous layer of the tuna mixture over the noodles. Continue alternating layers until all the ingredients are used up. You should have three layers of noodles and end with a layer of tuna mixture.
4. Top the casserole with the remaining ½ cup (50 g) each mozzarella and cheddar and loosely cover with aluminum foil. Bake for 40 minutes, then remove the foil and bake for another 10 minutes. Let stand for 10 minutes to firm up before cutting and serving.

USE WHAT YOU HAVE

INGREDIENT	TRY THIS INSTEAD:
Canned tuna	Canned chicken, leftover rotisserie chicken
Peas and carrots	Corn and broccoli
Cream of mushroom soup	Any condensed "cream of" soup
Lasagna noodles	1 cup dry macaroni

CREAMY MOCK CRAB PASTA

SERVES 3 TO 4

10 ounces (300 g) bowtie pasta or other similar shape such as large shells (not jumbo)*

1 tablespoon neutral oil

½ small onion, chopped

½ yellow bell pepper, chopped

4 white mushrooms, chopped

1 (8-ounce/250 g) package imitation crab

2 tablespoons butter

2 tablespoons all-purpose flour

1 cup (250 mL) milk

1 teaspoon dried parsley

½ teaspoon garlic powder

½ teaspoon salt, plus more to taste

¼ teaspoon pepper, plus more to taste

⅓ cup (75 g) cream cheese

*IF YOU'RE WORKING WITH A 1-POUND (454 G) PACKAGE OF PASTA, USE ABOUT TWO-THIRDS OF IT—CLOSE IS GOOD ENOUGH.

This one goes out to one of my old roommates' mom, who used to send him back to university with home-cooked meals. She graciously gave me the recipe, and even though I lost the card, I remembered the general method. So, here's my version of cream cheese pasta with imitation crab—aka hot dogs of the sea—which is much more affordable and accessible than real crabmeat.

1. Bring a large pot of lightly salted water to a boil and cook the pasta to al dente according to the package directions. Drain.
2. Meanwhile, heat the oil in a large skillet over medium heat. Add the onion, bell pepper, and mushrooms and sauté until the onion is slightly translucent, about 3 minutes. Add the phony crab, flattening the chunks with a spatula to lightly flake, and cook until the vegetables soften and the crab begins to brown, about 5 minutes. Transfer the vegetables and crab to a plate.
3. Melt the butter in the same pan, mix in the flour, and cook for a minute, then whisk in the milk, parsley, garlic powder, salt, and pepper until smooth. Add the cream cheese in chunks, mixing to incorporate. Add the cooked pasta, vegetables, and crab and mix to coat. Taste and adjust the salt and pepper if desired. Serve.

USE WHAT YOU HAVE

INGREDIENT	TRY THIS INSTEAD:
Imitation crab	Salad shrimp (the tiny ones), added toward the end so as not to overcook
Vegetables	Zucchini + summer squash

WHITE BEAN & SWEET POTATO MAC & CHEESE

SERVES 6 TO 8

1 tablespoon neutral oil

2 small sweet potatoes, peeled and sliced ¼ inch (6 mm) thick

½ medium onion, diced

3 garlic cloves, minced

1 (1-pound/454 g) package hearty pasta with ridges, such as cavatappi, penne, or lumaconi

1 (19-ounce/540 g) can white kidney beans (cannellini), rinsed and drained

2 teaspoons chicken bouillon

½ cup reserved pasta water

2 tablespoons butter

1 tablespoon all-purpose flour

½ teaspoon dried thyme

⅛ teaspoon ground nutmeg

½ cup (125 mL) cream or milk

1 teaspoon yellow mustard

Salt and pepper

1 cup (100 g) shredded mozzarella cheese

2 cups (200 g) shredded cheddar cheese, divided

Here's one from my popular "making my kids dinner with ingredients they hate" series, where I try to hide healthy ingredients in my kids' favorite foods. White beans and sweet potato become unrecognizable in this super creamy twist on a classic baked mac and cheese.

1. Preheat the oven to 350°F (175°C). Grease a 9 × 13-inch casserole dish with nonstick cooking spray.
2. Heat the oil in a large skillet over medium heat. Add the sweet potatoes and onion, cover, and cook, stirring every few minutes, until the sweet potatoes soften. Add the garlic and cook for a few minutes longer. If the sweet potatoes are browning before they soften, add a splash of water to help steam them.
3. Meanwhile, bring a large pot of lightly salted water to a boil and cook the pasta to just under al dente, about 6 minutes. Drain the pasta, reserving ½ cup of the pasta water. Dump the partially cooked pasta into the prepared casserole dish.
4. Add the sweet potatoes, onion, garlic, beans, bouillon, and reserved pasta water to a blender and blend until smooth.
5. Melt the butter in the same pan over medium-low heat, then stir in the flour, thyme, and nutmeg to incorporate. Cook for 1 minute, then whisk in the cream to make a roux. Once the roux begins to thicken, pour in the sweet potato mixture and stir to reheat. Add the mustard (even if you aren't a mustard lover, I wouldn't skip it—it gives the sauce the sharpness needed to balance the sweet potato), then sprinkle in the mozzarella and 1 cup (100 g) of the cheddar cheese, stirring well between each handful to avoid clumping. Taste and adjust the salt and pepper if desired.
6. Pour the sauce over the pasta and gently stir to coat. Top with the remaining 1 cup (100 g) cheddar cheese. Bake the casserole for about 10 minutes for the flavors to meld and the cheese to melt. Serve.

WHY: YOU WANT TO SLIGHTLY UNDERCOOK THE PASTA BECAUSE IT WILL KEEP COOKING AS IT BAKES, AND WE WANT TO AVOID MUSHY MAC AND CHEESE.

WHY: PASTA WATER IS FULL OF PASTA STARCH, WHICH HELPS THE SAUCE BIND TO THE PASTA.

BTW . . . YOU CAN PREPARE THIS DISH AHEAD AND REFRIGERATE IT OVERNIGHT BEFORE BAKING, BUT THE COOK TIME WILL INCREASE. FOR THE BEST RESULTS, PLACE THE CASSEROLE DISH IN THE OVEN WHILE PREHEATING. THIS WILL HELP PREVENT THERMAL SHOCK.

BETTER THAN BOXED INSTANT POT MAC & CHEESE

SERVES 4

1 (1-pound/454 g) package elbow macaroni

3½ cups (875 mL) water

1 teaspoon salt

½ teaspoon garlic powder

¼ cup (56 g) cream cheese

1 tablespoon butter

6 ounces (150 g) mozzarella cheese, shredded (about 1½ cups)*

6 ounces (150 g) cheddar cheese, shredded (about 1½ cups)*

¼ to ½ cup (60 to 125 mL) milk

I make this macaroni and cheese so often I could do it with my eyes closed. It is top requested by my kids and doesn't take any longer than boxed, and I almost always have these ingredients on hand, which means when we run out of lunch stuff, you can bet it'll be in their thermoses.

1. Add the macaroni, water, salt, and garlic powder to an electric pressure cooker. Secure the lid and cook for 4 minutes on high pressure, then open the quick release valve.
2. Once the pin drops, open the pressure cooker and stir in the cream cheese and butter. I usually close the lid again for a few minutes to let the cream cheese melt. Stir to incorporate, then add the shredded cheeses one handful at a time, stirring in between to prevent clumping. Add ¼ cup (60 mL) milk and stir, then add more milk if desired to reach the preferred creaminess. Serve.

ALTERNATIVE METHOD

You can also make this on the stovetop. Add the macaroni, water, salt, and garlic powder to a large skillet. Cover and bring to a boil, then reduce the heat and simmer until the pasta is cooked to al dente, about 8 minutes (pasta tends to take a bit longer to cook when you aren't fully submerging it). Stir the pasta every few minutes, adding more water as needed if it is absorbed before the pasta cooks through. Turn off the heat but leave the pan on the element and continue with step 2.

*IT'S IMPORTANT TO SHRED YOUR OWN CHEESE FOR THIS RECIPE. PRESHREDDED CHEESE HAS A COATING THAT JUST DOESN'T MELT AS WELL.

LEFTOVER SPAGHETTI PIE

SERVES 4 TO 6

2 packed cups leftover cooked spaghetti in sauce

1 cup (100 g) shredded mozzarella cheese

1 cup (100 g) shredded cheddar cheese

½ cup (50 g) grated Parmesan cheese

4 large eggs

1 teaspoon garlic powder

1 teaspoon onion powder

1 teaspoon dried parsley

1 teaspoon dried basil

½ teaspoon dried oregano

¼ teaspoon salt

¼ teaspoon pepper

1 to 2 tablespoons olive oil

It took me a few tries making this to get it to come out smoothly from the pan, so if yours doesn't, don't take it personally. It's worth trying again next time because it's *that good*! I like eating it in wedges, cold—it's perfect for a picnic. Feel free to switch up the sauce and cheese based on what you have; just keep the total amounts about the same.

1. Preheat the oven to 375°F (190°C).
2. Combine the leftover spaghetti, cheeses, eggs, garlic powder, onion powder, parsley, basil, oregano, salt, and pepper in a large bowl until combined.
3. Heat the oil in a medium oven-safe skillet (I use cast iron) over medium heat. Make sure the sides of the pan are also coated in oil to prevent sticking. **HOT TIP: I use a silicone brush to bring some oil up the sides. This step is important, because if the pan isn't well greased, you won't be able to get the pie out in one piece.**
4. Pour the spaghetti-egg mixture into the pan. Cover and cook for 3 minutes, then uncover, move to the oven, and bake for 20 minutes, or until the eggs are set. **HOT TIP: If your pan doesn't have a cover, you can use aluminum foil or lay a small baking sheet on top—be careful when you remove it as hot condensation can form on the baking sheet.**
5. Let the pie rest for 10 minutes before removing from the pan. I recommend using a silicone spatula to loosen the pie. Be sure the whole pie is separated from the pan, then flip it over onto a cutting board and cut into wedges to serve. If anything is stuck to the pan, it won't come out in one piece; if this happens, try slicing it in the pan and serving that way.

HIDDEN VEGGIE PASTA PRIMAVERA

SERVES 6

1 yellow onion, roughly chopped

1 red onion, roughly chopped

2 medium carrots, peeled and roughly chopped

1 red bell pepper, roughly chopped

6 white mushrooms, roughly chopped (optional)

3 garlic cloves, minced

2 teaspoons dried basil

Salt

2 tablespoons butter, cut into cubes

1 (24-ounce/680 mL) can or jar tomato sauce

2 teaspoons beef bouillon

1 teaspoon sugar

1 (1-pound/454 g) package rigatoni

I figured out you can just throw a random assortment of vegetables in the slow cooker and walk away, then blend them into sauce once they're caramelized. Clean out your veggie drawer with this pasta sauce and your kids will never know they're getting their five a day. Serve over pasta and top with Parmesan. This pairs well with Sneaky Turkey Meatballs (page 68).

1. Grease a slow cooker insert with nonstick cooking spray. Add the onions, carrots, bell pepper, mushrooms (if using), and garlic and sprinkle with the basil and salt to taste. Distribute the butter cubes over the vegetables. Cover and cook on high for 4 hours.
2. Add the tomato sauce, bouillon, and sugar. Cover and continue cooking for 2 hours longer for the flavors to develop.
3. Puree the vegetables using an immersion blender or allow them to cool a bit and then transfer to a blender to puree. **HOT TIP: When blending hot liquids, remove the center cap from the blender lid and hold a kitchen towel over the hole while blending to allow the steam to escape without blowing the lid off.**
4. Bring a large pot of lightly salted water to a boil and cook the pasta according to the package directions. Drain, reserving ½ cup pasta water. Mix the reserved pasta water and ½ cup (125 mL) of the pasta sauce into the rigatoni to coat. Serve the pasta topped with the additional sauce.

WHY: SAUCING UP THE NOODLES HELPS KEEP THEM FROM STICKING TOGETHER AND HELPS THE SAUCE STICK TO THE PASTA BETTER.

DO'S AND DON'TS FOR CHOOSING VEGGIES

DO use vegetables that already have some sweetness in them, such as carrots, sweet bell peppers, and onions—ask yourself: If I roasted them long enough, would they caramelize?

DON'T use cruciferous vegetables, like broccoli and cabbage. These will give the sauce a bitter undertone.

SHEET PAN GNOCCHI

SERVES 3 TO 4

2 tablespoons nutritional yeast* (optional but recommended)
1 teaspoon garlic powder
1 teaspoon onion powder
1 teaspoon dried oregano
½ teaspoon pepper
1 (1-pound/500 g) package shelf-stable potato gnocchi
2 tablespoons olive oil, divided
4 cups (300 g) broccoli florets
½ teaspoon salt

*NUTRITIONAL YEAST IS AN INGREDIENT OFTEN USED IN VEGAN FOOD TO MAKE IT TASTE "CHEESY." IT CAN BE FOUND IN THE HEALTH FOOD SECTION OF THE GROCERY STORE OR IN BULK FOOD STORES.

Did you know you can bake gnocchi? I buy shelf-stable potato gnocchi at a fraction of the cost of fresh or frozen, making this a super affordable convenience meal. (It's also great as a side dish with chicken or salmon.) My local stores typically stock it either in the pasta aisle on the lower shelf, or in the international aisle. This kind tends to be on the salty side (perhaps because it's typically boiled), so salt cautiously and add more after serving if needed. Check out page 63 for more sheet pan dinner ideas.

1. Preheat the oven to 400°F (200°C). Line a rimmed baking sheet with parchment paper.
2. Combine the nutritional yeast, garlic powder, onion powder, oregano, and pepper in a small bowl. Transfer half of the seasoning mix to a large bowl, add the gnocchi and 1 tablespoon of the olive oil, and stir to coat. Spread in a single layer on one side of the lined baking sheet.
3. Add the broccoli, remaining 1 tablespoon olive oil, remaining seasoning mix, and salt to the same large bowl and stir to coat. Spread in a single layer on the other side of the baking sheet. **HOT TIP: The reason you're keeping the ingredients separate is in case one starts to cook faster than the other, you'll be able to easily transfer to a plate and return the other ingredient to the oven to finish.**
4. Bake for 15 to 20 minutes, until the gnocchi are lightly golden on the outside and pillowy on the inside, and the broccoli is starting to crisp but is not burned. Serve.

BTW . . . YOU CAN SWAP FROZEN BROCCOLI IF THAT'S MORE AFFORDABLE OR ACCESSIBLE FOR YOU—BE SURE THE BAG YOU HAVE IS LABELED "FLORETS"; THE ONE LABELED "CHOPPED" IS MOSTLY STEMS AND IS A BETTER CHOICE FOR BOILED APPLICATIONS.

LATE-NIGHT RAMEN

SERVES 2 TO 3

1 tablespoon neutral oil

8 ounces (227 g) white mushrooms, chopped

½ medium onion, chopped, *or* ½ cup (75 g) frozen chopped onion

1 cup (150 g) chopped fresh or frozen vegetables of choice

2 garlic cloves, minced

3 (2.46-ounce/70 g) packages Maggi ramen noodles

2 cups (500 mL) water

¼ cup cream cheese

2 tablespoons ketchup

This is one of those recipes where you're just going to have to trust me. Maggi noodles (masala flavor) were recommended to me on TikTok and when I tried them, people suggested adding cream cheese and ketchup. I'm not even sure if I was supposed to add both at the same time, but I will say this unusual combo hits the spot and you have to try it!

1. Heat the oil in a large nonstick skillet over medium heat. Add the mushrooms, onion, and chopped vegetables and cook, stirring frequently, until everything softens, 8 to 10 minutes. Add the garlic and cook for 2 to 3 minutes longer.
2. Add the noodles and water, reserving the seasoning packets. Cover and bring to a boil, then uncover, break apart the noodles, and cook until soft, about 2 minutes.
3. Mix in the seasoning packets, then stir in the cream cheese to melt and incorporate. Finally mix in the ketchup. Serve.

PEANUT BUTTER STIR-FRY NOODLES

SERVES 4

1 (14-ounce/400 g) package rice noodles, preferably wide

1½ tablespoons neutral oil, divided

6 cups sliced vegetables or frozen stir-fry mix

4 garlic cloves, minced

2-inch (5 cm) piece ginger, peeled and minced

¼ cup (60 mL) soy sauce

½ cup (135 g) smooth peanut butter

¼ to ½ cup (60 to 125 mL) hot water

2 tablespoons honey

1 tablespoon apple cider vinegar or seasoned rice vinegar

2 teaspoons toasted sesame oil

1 tablespoon sriracha (optional)

4 large eggs

Chopped fresh cilantro, sliced green onions, and/or lime wedges, to garnish (optional)

BTW . . . IF YOU LIKE YOUR NOODLES REALLY SAUCY AND LESS PAD THAI–ADJACENT, YOU CAN MAKE 1.5 TIMES THE SAUCE.

This recipe started as a spin-off from pad Thai and evolved into one of my biggest comfort meals. I found it tricky to shop for one when I was in university, so I always had odds and ends of veggies to use up. Thinly slice whatever needs to be cooked (onions, green beans, bell peppers, snow peas, etc.) or grab a bag of frozen mixed veggies to save on prep time.

1. Soak the rice noodles in warm water for 10 to 15 minutes, until softened (time will depend on the thickness of the noodles), then drain. **HOT TIP: Some rice noodle packages say to soak in boiling water, but using warm water helps them stick together less, although it will take longer.**
2. Meanwhile, heat 1 tablespoon of the neutral oil in a wok or large skillet over medium heat. Add the vegetables, garlic, and ginger and sauté, stirring occasionally, until slightly softened but still a bit crisp, 4 to 5 minutes. The cook time will depend on whether you used fresh or frozen vegetables and how thinly you sliced them.
3. Whisk together the soy sauce, peanut butter, ¼ cup (60 mL) hot water, honey, vinegar, sesame oil, and sriracha (if using) in a small bowl. If the peanut butter won't fully integrate, you can microwave it for 15 seconds.
4. Add the softened noodles and sauce to the wok, gently stirring to coat. If the sauce is too thick, add up to another ¼ cup (60 mL) hot water to thin the sauce a bit.
5. Heat the remaining ½ tablespoon neutral oil in a large nonstick skillet over medium heat. Crack the eggs into the skillet, cover, and cook until the whites are set and the yolks are still runny, 3 to 4 minutes. **HOT TIP: To get "prettier" eggs, you can cook them uncovered over medium-low heat.** Over-easy is also fine—whatever you are most comfortable with.
6. To serve, divide the noodles and vegetables into bowls and top each with an egg. Optionally, garnish with more sriracha, green onions, cilantro, and a lime wedge.

USE WHAT YOU HAVE

INGREDIENT	TRY THIS INSTEAD:
Rice noodles	Ramen noodles or spaghetti
Eggs	Tofu, chicken, shrimp
Smooth peanut butter	Chunky peanut butter (avoid using natural nut butters, as they don't dissolve into the sauce as well and are typically unsweetened)
Honey	Brown sugar
Apple cider vinegar	Seasoned rice vinegar (this is actually ideal, but more people have ACV on hand) OR White vinegar (start with 2 teaspoons and adjust to taste)
Toasted sesame oil	Recommended but can be omitted—we are using it for flavor, not fat

MUSHROOM HOISIN UDON

SERVES 4

1 tablespoon neutral oil

8 ounces (227 g) white mushrooms, sliced

8 ounces (227 g) cremini mushrooms, sliced

1 tablespoon minced ginger

4 garlic cloves, minced

4 (6-ounce/200 g) packages udon noodles

½ cup (125 mL) chicken broth

¼ cup (60 mL) hoisin sauce

2 tablespoons low-sodium soy sauce

2 tablespoons dark soy sauce

1 teaspoon toasted sesame oil

Sliced green onions, for serving

Mushrooms are really out here saying "Forget the meat, you don't need it!" I keep a package of udon in the cupboard so I can make this recipe when I need to get supper on the table fast but didn't really plan ahead. Note that not all udon is created equal—I've had some that tasted a bit like Play-Doh smells, so if you're trying a new brand, taste the noodles beforehand.

1. Heat the neutral oil in a large skillet or wok over medium heat. Add the mushrooms and sauté, stirring occasionally, for 5 minutes. Add the ginger and continue cooking until the mushrooms are soft, about 5 minutes more. Add the garlic and cook for a few more minutes.
2. Meanwhile, bring a large pot of lightly salted water to a boil and cook the udon according to the package directions. Drain. In a small bowl, mix together the broth, hoisin sauce, soy sauces, and sesame oil.
3. Add the udon and sauce to the pan with the mushrooms and stir to coat. Continue cooking until the sauce thickens and sticks to the noodles, about 3 minutes. Serve topped with green onions.

WHY: GARLIC COOKS FAST, AND BURNT GARLIC IS BITTER, SO WE WANT TO AVOID THAT.

USE WHAT YOU HAVE

INGREDIENT	TRY THIS INSTEAD:
White and cremini mushrooms	OK to use all one kind; this is also great with chicken
Dark soy sauce	OK to use all regular soy sauce; it won't be as glossy or dark and will have a milder flavor

CHAPTER THREE

SOUPS, STEWS & SKILLETS

Soups, stews, and skillets are the ultimate ingredient stretchers: Throw bits of meat and the veggies wilting in the bottom of your crisper into a pot together and you end up with a rich, hearty, flavorful meal. The recipes in this section are one-pot and beginner-friendly, perfect for those days you just need to turn your brain off. No fancy techniques—just chop, sauté, and maybe simmer. You've got this!

ACADIAN FRICOT

SERVES 6 TO 8

SOUP

1 tablespoon neutral oil

1 medium onion, cut into ¼-inch (6 mm) pieces

2 celery ribs, cut into ¼-inch (6 mm) pieces

3 garlic cloves, minced

¼ rutabaga, peeled and cut into ¼-inch (6 mm) chunks

2 large carrots, peeled and sliced ¼ inch (6 mm) thick

2 large white potatoes*, scrubbed and cut into ½-inch (2 cm) chunks

3 boneless, skinless chicken breasts, cooked and shredded, *or* ½ rotisserie chicken, skin and bones removed and meat shredded

2 (1-quart/900 mL) cartons chicken broth or homemade chicken broth

1½ tablespoons dried summer savory

½ teaspoon salt

½ teaspoon pepper

DUMPLINGS

1 cup (125 g) all-purpose flour

2 teaspoons baking powder

½ teaspoon salt

½ cup very cold water

If you've never learned Acadian history, it is worth a read! (BTW: The 1755 deportation is how Cajuns landed in Louisiana.) In francophone schools in New Brunswick, Acadian music, celebrations, and food were always at the forefront. I was a cafeteria kid, and they used to serve fricot (the Acadian version of chicken and dumpling stew) as the lunch option a few times per month—you'd get not one but *two* bowls of this simple but hearty meal!

It's the dried summer savory that sets this recipe apart from other versions of chicken and dumplings; it's readily available in Canada, but if you can't get it, I recommend using mostly dried marjoram with a bit of thyme and oregano.

---

1. Heat the oil in a large pot or Dutch oven over medium heat. Add the onion and celery and sauté, stirring often, until slightly translucent, about 5 minutes. Add the garlic and cook for another few minutes to soften.
2. Add the rutabaga, carrots, potatoes, chicken, broth, summer savory, salt, and pepper and bring to a light boil. Reduce to a simmer and cook for 20 to 30 minutes, until all the vegetables are fork-tender.
3. Meanwhile, make the dumpling dough: Mix together the flour, baking powder, and salt in a small bowl. Stir in the cold water until a dough forms.
4. Bring the soup back up to a low boil and drop in clumps of dumpling dough (I prefer smaller dumplings, 1 teaspoon in size, but make them to your preference). Work in batches and stir the soup when you get a semi-covered top layer so they don't stick together. Cook for 3 to 5 minutes, until the dumplings are cooked through. Let cool for at least 10 minutes before serving as the soup will be extremely hot.

* YOU CAN USE YELLOW OR RED POTATOES IN PLACE OF WHITE. I DON'T RECOMMEND USING RUSSET AS I PERSONALLY FIND THEY GET A MEALY TEXTURE WHEN BOILED.

BTW . . . IT'S IMPORTANT TO CUT THE DIFFERENT VEGETABLES IN SIZES THAT WILL COOK IN APPROXIMATELY THE SAME AMOUNT OF TIME.

ALTERNATIVE METHOD

You can also make it in an electric pressure cooker: Sauté the onion, celery, garlic, rutabaga, and carrots on Sauté mode, then add the potatoes, chicken, broth, summer savory, salt, and pepper. Pressure cook on high for 5 minutes, then natural release. Turn back to Sauté on high and make the dumplings as in steps 3 and 4.

CREAMY CHICKEN TACO SOUP

SERVES 4

1 tablespoon neutral oil

½ yellow onion, finely diced

3 garlic cloves, minced

½ bell pepper (any color), chopped

2 tablespoons tomato paste

1 tablespoon chili powder

1 teaspoon ground cumin

1 teaspoon dried oregano

½ teaspoon salt

¼ teaspoon pepper

1 (19-ounce/540 g) can black beans or red kidney beans, rinsed and drained

1½ cups (225 g) frozen corn kernels

2 cups (280 g) cooked shredded chicken, such as leftover rotisserie chicken

1 (28-ounce/794 g) can diced tomatoes

1 (1-quart/900 mL) carton chicken broth

¼ cup (30 g) cream cheese

When I was growing up, my house did not have the flavors of the world—it didn't even have the flavors of a taco kit! The first time I tried a taco I was *fifteen*. Taco soup is now a family favorite, and it's all about the toppings. Scrounge your refrigerator and pantry to load it up for the ultimate experience. (Bonus: Using what you have reduces food waste and saves you money!) Typical toppings include avocado, fresh cilantro, sour cream, shredded cheese, tortilla chips, and lime, but you don't need all of them at once.

1. Heat the oil in a heavy-bottomed pot (or in an electric pressure cooker) over medium heat. Add the onion, garlic, and bell pepper and sauté, stirring, for a few minutes, until the onion softens. Add the tomato paste, chili powder, cumin, oregano, salt, and pepper and sauté for another minute to develop the flavors.
2. Add the beans, corn, chicken, tomatoes with their juice, and broth. Season to taste with salt and pepper.
3. Bring to a boil, then reduce to a simmer and cook for 20 minutes (or run the electric pressure cooker for 5 minutes on high, then natural release). Add the cream cheese and gently stir until combined. Serve with your toppings of choice.

GO-TO SAUSAGE SOUP

SERVES 4

1 tablespoon neutral oil

3 Italian sausages, removed from casings

1 medium onion, chopped

2 celery ribs, chopped

1 large carrot, peeled and chopped

2 garlic cloves, minced

3 medium white, red, or yellow potatoes, scrubbed and chopped*

1 (28-ounce/794 g) can diced tomatoes, or other canned tomatoes

⅓ cup (65 g) red lentils

1 (1-quart/900 mL) carton chicken broth

2 bay leaves

1 teaspoon Italian seasoning

¼ teaspoon salt

⅛ teaspoon pepper

2 cups (60 g) baby spinach (see Tip)

1 cup (250 mL) heavy cream

*NO NEED TO PEEL THE POTATOES, IMO, BUT YOU DO YOU.

This sausage soup is a family favorite—and budget friendly because it uses only three sausages. You still get that meat flavor with less, but it's hearty because we backfill it with affordable ingredients like red lentils and potatoes. Serve with fresh dinner rolls.

1. Turn the electric pressure cooker to Sauté mode on medium heat and drizzle in the oil. Add the sausage meat and sauté, breaking up the meat as you cook, until it is no longer pink, about 8 minutes. Add the onion, celery, carrot, and garlic and sauté for about 5 minutes, until they start to soften. Add the potatoes, tomatoes with their juice, lentils, broth, bay leaves, Italian seasoning, salt, and pepper.
2. Lock the lid and set to pressure cook for 5 minutes on high, then let release naturally for at least 10 minutes before opening.
3. Stir in the spinach and cream, unplug the pressure cooker, and rest the lid back on top (you cannot rest the lid while it's on) for 3 minutes for the spinach to wilt and the cream to heat through before serving.

ALTERNATIVE METHOD

To make this on the stovetop, follow step 1, but use a large, heavy-bottomed pot. For step 2, bring to a boil, then reduce to a simmer and cook for 20 minutes, or until the lentils and potatoes are cooked through. Continue with step 3.

BTW . . . IF YOU, LIKE ME, NEVER FINISH A FULL PACKAGE OF FRESH BABY SPINACH, TOSS THE REMAINDER IN THE FREEZER (RIGHT IN ITS ORIGINAL PACKAGING IF YOU HAVE SPACE, OR TRANSFER TO A ZIPPER-TOP BAG). RECIPES LIKE THIS ONE WHERE YOU'RE COOKING DOWN THE SPINACH ANYWAY ARE THE PERFECT WAY TO USE UP FROZEN SPINACH.

PIZZA SOUP

SERVES 4

1 tablespoon neutral oil

1 medium onion, diced

1 celery rib, diced

1 medium carrot, peeled and diced

8 ounces (227 g) white mushrooms, diced

1 tablespoon minced garlic

5 ounces (150 g) chopped pepperoni or salami

1 (6-ounce/170 g) can tomato paste

1 tablespoon Italian seasoning

1 (1-quart/900 mL) carton chicken broth

1 teaspoon sugar

1 (12-ounce/350 g) package fresh cheese tortellini

1 lemon wedge (optional)

2 cups (200 g) shredded mozzarella cheese

My kids always get excited for pizza soup, and they don't need to know I only make it because I have a fridge full of slightly sad veggies and abandoned leftovers. This is the ultimate We Use What We Have recipe—never the same but always a favorite. I typically make it in my Instant Pot because I love hands-off cooking, but I've included stovetop instructions too.

1. Heat the oil in an electric pressure cooker set to Sauté mode or in a large, heavy-bottomed pot over medium heat. Add the onion, celery, carrot, mushrooms, garlic, and pepperoni and sauté until they begin to soften, about 5 minutes. Add the tomato paste and Italian seasoning and sauté for another few minutes to bring out their flavors.
2. Add the broth and sugar. Set the pressure cook for 5 minutes on high, then let naturally release for 10 minutes. If using the stovetop, bring to a boil, then reduce to a simmer for 20 minutes.
3. Turn the pressure cooker back to Sauté mode. Add the tortellini and cook for 5 minutes. Optionally, add a squeeze of lemon juice for zing. Top individual bowls with cheese—it's pizza soup, after all!

BTW . . . THIS RECIPE IS MORE OF A FORMULA FOR MY "CLEAN OUT THE FRIDGE" SOUP, SO FEEL FREE TO EXPERIMENT WITH IT! GRAB EVERYTHING THAT'S BEEN SITTING AROUND—FLOPPY VEGETABLES, MEAL PREP THAT NEVER GOT USED, LEFTOVERS NOBODY IS REACHING FOR. INSPECT EVERYTHING TO MAKE SURE IT'S STILL EDIBLE AND FOOD SAFE (SEE PAGE 23 FOR MORE INFO). AND YOU CAN USE MORE OR LESS PASTA AND IT WILL STILL TURN OUT FINE.

continues

USE WHAT YOU HAVE

TOMATO PASTE	PROTEIN	VEGETABLES	STARCH/CARB
Tomato sauce (use 1 cup, reduce broth to 4 cups)	Rotisserie chicken	Vegetable crudités	Pasta, cooked or dry
Pasta sauce (use 1 cup, reduce broth to 4 cups, skip the sugar, and halve the seasonings)	Ground meat/ taco meat	Frozen/canned vegetables	Rice, cooked or dry
Condensed tomato soup (use 2 cans, reduce broth to 4 cups, and skip the sugar)	Meatballs/ sausage	Leftover cooked vegetables	Potatoes, cooked or fresh
Canned tomatoes (soup won't be as rich; reduce broth by size of can used)	Boiled eggs	Avoid using vegetables that aren't typically served cooked	Leftover one-pan meal, like a pasta dish
Canned vegetable soup	Canned beans	Canned vegetable soup	Avoid using mayonnaise-based leftovers like potato or pasta salad

CURRY SWEET POTATO SOUP

SERVES 4 TO 6

1 tablespoon neutral oil
1 medium onion, chopped
3 garlic cloves, minced
1 tablespoon curry powder
4 to 5 medium sweet potatoes, peeled and cubed
1 cup (200 g) red lentils
½ teaspoon salt
1 (1-quart/900 mL) carton chicken broth
1 (14-ounce/400 mL) can coconut milk
Juice of ½ lime, plus 1 lime cut into wedges
Crushed peanuts, for topping
Chopped fresh cilantro, for topping (optional)

Curry sweet potato soup is always first on my list when the weather turns cool. I created this recipe in my lentil era, aka that time I was sneaking lentils into every meal (hello, cheap protein and fiber!). It's quick and freezes well so you can portion it out for future lunches too. I make it in my electric pressure cooker, but I've also included stovetop instructions.

1. Heat the oil in an electric pressure cooker on Sauté mode set to medium. Add the onion and cook, stirring often, until translucent, about 3 minutes. Add the garlic and sauté for a few minutes, then add the curry powder and cook for another minute to release the aroma. Add the sweet potatoes, lentils, salt, and broth and set to pressure cook for 8 minutes on high, then natural release for 10 minutes.
2. Using an immersion blender, puree the soup. **QUICK TIP: You can use a standard blender or food processor to puree, but you will need to let the soup cool a bit first.** Alternatively, leave it chunky if you prefer. Mix in the coconut milk and the juice of ½ lime. **HOT TIP: Microwaving citrus fruits for a few seconds makes them easier to juice.** Serve topped with crushed peanuts and chopped cilantro, if desired, and a lime wedge.

ALTERNATIVE METHOD

To make this on the stovetop, use a large, heavy-bottomed pot or Dutch oven. After sautéing the vegetables, add the lentils, broth, and coconut milk, bring the soup to a boil, then reduce to a simmer and cook until the lentils and sweet potatoes are very soft, about 15 minutes. Continue with step 2.

KID-APPROVED FISH SOUP

SERVES 4

2 tablespoons butter

1 tablespoon neutral oil

½ medium yellow onion, diced

2 celery ribs, diced

2 carrots, peeled and diced

2 garlic cloves, minced

2 medium potatoes, any kind, peeled and diced

1 cup (150 g) frozen corn kernels

1 pound (454 g) white fish such as haddock

2 teaspoons dried thyme

2 teaspoons Old Bay Seasoning

3 cups (750 mL) chicken broth

1 tablespoon cornstarch

½ cup (125 mL) heavy cream or evaporated milk

Salt and pepper

If there's one leftover ingredient I really struggle to repurpose, it's fish, but it's too expensive to waste. This soup is flexible whether you have fresh, frozen, or leftover fish (for food safety, I recommend using leftover fish within 2 days). You can make it in an electric pressure cooker or on the stovetop. It is meant to be chunky and hearty, so if you don't have much fish you can increase the potatoes or reduce the broth to make up for it. I like to do a double clean-out by serving it with toasted artisan bread since I usually have half a loaf of something in the freezer.

---

1. Melt the butter and oil together in an electric pressure cooker set to Sauté mode over medium heat or in a large, heavy-bottomed pot on the stovetop. Add the onion, celery, carrots, and garlic and sauté, stirring often, for 5 minutes.
2. Add the potatoes, corn, fish, thyme, Old Bay, and broth. **HOT TIP: The Old Bay Seasoning really makes this, but you can find recipes online to mix up your own if you don't want to buy it.** Close the lid and set to pressure cook on high for 5 minutes, then let the pressure release naturally. If cooking on the stovetop, bring to a boil, then reduce the heat and simmer for 15 minutes, or until the vegetables and fish are cooked through.
3. Turn Sauté mode back on the pressure cooker and sprinkle the cornstarch into the soup, stirring constantly to prevent clumping. **HOT TIP: Best practice is to mix cornstarch into a bit of cold water, but I cut corners and it's always fine.** Cook for another few minutes, until the soup begins to thicken. Stir in the cream, season with salt and pepper to taste, and serve.

BTW . . . YOU CAN MAKE THIS WITH ANY POTATO, EVEN A SWEET POTATO IF THAT'S WHAT YOU HAVE ON HAND.

CABBAGE NO-ROLL STEW

SERVES 4

2 cups (400 g) white rice

1 tablespoon olive oil

1 pound (454 g) ground beef

1 medium onion, finely chopped

½ small head cabbage, chopped into ¾-inch (2 cm) squares (about 6 cups)

3 garlic cloves, minced

1 (28-ounce/794 g) can diced tomatoes

2 teaspoons Worcestershire sauce

2 teaspoons beef bouillon

2 teaspoons dried oregano

1 teaspoon dried thyme

¼ teaspoon pepper

1 (10-ounce/284 mL) can condensed tomato soup

Salt

Once in a blue moon when I was growing up, my grandma would make cabbage rolls and I devoured them. As an adult I totally get why they weren't part of the regular rotation even though the ingredients are pretty affordable—*so many steps*. Who's got time for that?! Now I make a deconstructed version that's much less effort but just as comforting. Serve over white rice.

1. Cook the rice according to the package directions.
2. Meanwhile, heat the oil in a Dutch oven or large, heavy-bottomed pot over medium heat. Cook the beef, stirring to break up the meat, until browned, about 7 minutes. If the beef has a lot of grease, you can make a well in the middle of the pot and soak some up with a paper towel. Add the onion, cabbage, and garlic and sauté until the onion is translucent, about 5 minutes. Add the tomatoes with their juice, Worcestershire, bouillon, oregano, thyme, and pepper.
3. Cover and bring to a boil, then reduce to a simmer and cook until the cabbage is soft, about 20 minutes. Trust me: I know it looks dry, but there's is no need to add extra liquid; since we are cooking the stew covered, the cabbage and tomatoes will release enough liquid to form the sauce. Mix in the tomato soup and continue cooking for about 5 minutes to let the flavors meld. Season with salt to taste. Serve the stew in bowls over the rice.

WHY: ONIONS WILL SWEAT AND RELEASE LIQUID, SO YOU WANT TO DRAIN THE MEAT BEFOREHAND, RATHER THAN AFTER WHEN YOU'LL END UP LOSING THAT DELICIOUS ONION JUICE.

WHY: IT'S IMPORTANT TO WAIT UNTIL THE END OF COOKING TO ADD THE CONDENSED TOMATO SOUP BECAUSE IT HAS SUGAR, AND SUGAR TENDS TO BURN.

USE WHAT YOU HAVE

INGREDIENT	TRY THIS INSTEAD:
Ground beef	Ground pork
Diced tomatoes + tomato soup	Tomato sauce + sugar (add 1 teaspoon at a time, to taste)
Worcestershire	1 teaspoon soy sauce + 1 teaspoon sugar

ENCORE DU STEW

SERVES 4 TO 6

STEW

⅓ cup (40 g) all-purpose flour

1 teaspoon salt

½ teaspoon pepper

2 pounds (1 kg) stewing beef cubes, or beef cut into bite-size cubes

1 tablespoon neutral oil

2 tablespoons tomato paste

1 teaspoon balsamic vinegar

1 teaspoon dried thyme

1 medium onion, chopped

2 celery ribs, sliced

3 carrots, peeled and chopped

3 garlic cloves, minced

1 (1-quart/900 mL) carton beef broth

MASHED POTATOES*

6 russet potatoes, scrubbed and cubed (We like peels in our mash—plus they have extra nutrients—but you can peel.)

¼ cup (60 g) butter

¼ cup (60 mL) milk

Salt and pepper

GRAVY

2 tablespoons all-purpose flour

¼ cup (60 mL) water

Growing up, I often heard the story about how my grandmother would make beef stew every Sunday. Her recipe used a brown gravy mix that's basically cornstarch and bouillon, so I set out to replace that with pantry ingredients, and my aunt later made a version over mashed potatoes that stretches the meal even further. My mom had four sisters and they would all invite their boyfriends over for dinner, so they used to joke, "Encore du stew?!" . . . Anyway, yes, stew again.

---

1. Mix together the flour, salt, and pepper in a medium bowl. Pat the beef cubes dry with a paper towel, then toss in the flour mixture to coat. Heat the oil in a Dutch oven or other heavy-bottomed pot over medium heat. Add the beef cubes and sear for 2 to 3 minutes per side, until all sides are browned.
2. Add the tomato paste, balsamic vinegar, and thyme and cook for 2 minutes to develop flavors, then add the onion, celery, carrots, garlic, and broth. Scrape the bottom of the pot to incorporate any crispy bits, *ahem* flavor. Cover and bring to a boil, then reduce the heat to low and leave to simmer for at least 40 minutes.
3. Meanwhile, put the potatoes in a medium saucepan, cover with cold water, and lightly salt. Bring to a boil and cook until the potatoes are fork-tender, 10 to 15 minutes. Drain the potatoes, return them to the pan, add the butter and milk, and mash. Taste and adjust by adding more milk, salt, and pepper as desired.

*IF YOU'RE SHORT ON POTATOES OR DON'T HAVE BUTTER AND MILK, SKIP THE MASH AND ADD CUBED POTATOES RIGHT INTO THE STEW WHEN YOU ADD THE CARROTS—YOU MAY NEED TO INCREASE THE BROTH A BIT TO COVER.

continues

ALTERNATIVE METHOD

You can also make this in the slow cooker. I recommend still searing the beef cubes for more depth of flavor, then add them to the slow cooker along with the vegetables, tomato paste, balsamic vinegar, thyme, and broth. Cover and cook on high for 4 hours or on low for 8, checking on it halfway as slow cooker temperatures can vary.

4. To make the gravy, whisk the flour into the water until smooth. Pour the mixture into the beef stew and stir to combine. Bring the heat back up to a light boil and cook for a few minutes, until the gravy begins to thicken. Serve the stew over the mashed potatoes.

BTW . . . STEW BEEF IS JUST BEEF CUBES. USUALLY THESE ARE MADE UP FROM THE BIGGER PIECES OF BEEF TRIMMINGS WHEN BUTCHERS ARE CUTTING STEAKS, ROASTS, ETC., SO THEY END UP BEING MORE AFFORDABLE THAT WHOLE CUTS. IF ANOTHER CUT IS PRICED LOWER PER POUND, JUST GRAB THAT AND CUBE IT YOURSELF.

MASHED POTATO BOWLS

SERVES 4

4 cups leftover mashed potatoes, such as the ones from Encore du Stew (page 117)

2 cups (300 g) chopped cooked chicken or pork (optional)

2 cups (300 g) frozen corn kernels or simple vegetable mix

3 tablespoons butter

3 tablespoons all-purpose flour

1 teaspoon chicken bouillon

1 teaspoon beef bouillon

½ teaspoon garlic powder

½ teaspoon onion powder

¼ teaspoon dried thyme

¼ teaspoon pepper

1½ cups (375 mL) water

These takeout-inspired (think fried chicken restaurant) mashed potato bowls are the perfect home cooked-meets-convenience meal and one of my favorite ways to use up leftovers from a meat and potatoes dinner. Plus, the gravy recipe is super simple, using ingredients you probably have in your pantry, and it even works as a meatless meal.

---

1. Reheat the leftover mashed potatoes, meat (if using), and corn individually in the microwave.
2. In a small saucepan, melt the butter over medium-low heat. Mix in the flour and cook for 2 minutes, then whisk in the chicken and beef bouillon, garlic powder, onion powder, thyme, pepper, and water. Turn the heat up to medium and cook, stirring constantly, until the gravy thickens, about 2 minutes.
3. Divide the mashed potatoes, meat (if using), and corn into bowls. Spoon the gravy on top and serve.

PANEER & VEGETABLE KORMA

SERVES 4 TO 6

- 1 (10-ounce/300 g) block paneer, cut into 1-inch (2.5 cm) cubes
- 2 cups (200 g) basmati rice
- 1 tablespoon neutral oil
- ½ medium onion, chopped
- 4 cups (1 pound/454 g) chopped/shredded vegetables, such as broccoli slaw, cauliflower, carrots, eggplant
- 3 garlic cloves, minced
- 1 inch (2.5 cm) piece ginger, peeled and minced
- 1 (6-ounce/170 g) can tomato paste
- 1 tablespoon curry powder
- 1 teaspoon ground cumin
- ¼ teaspoon ground cinnamon
- ¼ teaspoon pepper
- ¼ teaspoon salt
- 1½ to 2 cups (375 to 500 mL) chicken broth
- 1 (14-ounce/400 mL) can coconut milk
- Chopped fresh cilantro, to garnish (optional)

I love a good curry, and when I learned how much protein there is in paneer (Indian cheese) I knew I had to find ways to incorporate it. You can substitute protein-rich halloumi—or even chickpeas—if you can't find paneer. My kids are a bit spice-averse, so I typically assume these types of meals are just for me, but even my three-year-old enjoyed this dish!

---

1. Put the paneer cubes in a heatproof bowl. Pour boiling water over the paneer to cover. Let sit for 10 to 15 minutes, then drain. Meanwhile, cook the rice according to the package directions.
2. Heat the oil in a Dutch oven or other large, heavy-bottomed pot over medium heat. Add the onion and sauté until translucent, then add the vegetables, garlic, and ginger and sauté for a few more minutes. Add the drained paneer, tomato paste, curry powder, cumin, cinnamon, salt, and pepper and cook for a few more minutes to develop the flavors. Add enough broth for the vegetables to be halfway submerged (the amount will depend on the size of your pot and how big you chopped the vegetables), reduce the heat to a simmer, and cook for 10 to 15 minutes, or until the vegetables are soft.
3. Stir in the coconut milk and cook for another minute to heat it up. Serve garnished with cilantro, if desired.

USE WHAT YOU HAVE

INGREDIENT	TRY THIS INSTEAD:
Paneer	Chickpeas
Chicken broth	Veggie broth, bouillon + water; avoid beef flavor, which is deeper/richer
Basmati rice	Any rice, or switch it up with ramen (you can cook it directly in the sauce, though you may need to add a bit of water)
Curry powder + cumin + cinnamon	1 tablespoon garam masala (won't be the same but will be delicious), plus ¼ to ½ teaspoon ground turmeric if you want it yellow
Coconut milk	Heavy cream or plain Greek yogurt. Start with ½ cup and adjust to taste. Again, it won't taste the same but will be delicious.

HOT DOG HASH BROWN SKILLET

SERVES 4

3 medium russet or other white-fleshed potatoes, scrubbed and sliced ¼ inch (6 mm) thick

¼ cup (60 mL) water

2 tablespoons neutral oil

1 medium onion, diced

½ green bell pepper, diced

½ red bell pepper, diced

3 white mushrooms, diced

6 hot dogs, sliced ½-inch (1 cm) thick

2 teaspoons garlic powder

1 teaspoon dried oregano

½ teaspoon smoked paprika

½ teaspoon salt, plus more to taste

¼ teaspoon pepper, plus more to taste

4 to 6 large eggs

Ketchup, for serving

Somehow even bologna has gotten pretty expensive! But it's basically a glorified hot dog, and store-brand chicken wieners remain very affordable. This skillet is one of my most budget-friendly, kid-friendly (feel free to skip the veg if your kids don't like them), and beginner cook–friendly recipes. The biggest limitation will be the size of your largest skillet—so feel free to halve this recipe or use two pans. Skip the eggs if you don't have them—it'll read more dinner and less breakfast but still feels like a complete meal.

---

1. Combine the potatoes and water in a large saucepan over medium heat and steam, uncovered, to soften the potatoes a bit, about 3 minutes. As soon as the water evaporates, mix in the oil so the potatoes don't stick to the pan. Add the onion, bell peppers, mushrooms, and hot dogs and sauté for 10 to 20 minutes, stirring occasionally to allow the potatoes to crisp but not burn. The time will depend on the size of your pan; if the pan is crowded, it will take longer to cook and crisp up.

2. Mix in the garlic powder, oregano, smoked paprika, salt, and pepper. Crack the eggs directly over the potato mixture. (I use one egg per person.) Cover the pan and cook until the yolks are the desired doneness—I like medium yolks best, which takes 5 to 7 minutes. If you don't have a cover for the pan, you can place a baking sheet on top. **HOT TIP: Use an oven mitt to take the baking sheet off and be careful as very hot water droplets will have formed under the sheet due to condensation.** Serve with ketchup.

BTW: I JUST SCRUB MY POTATOES—I LOVE A CRISPY POTATO SKIN—BUT YOU ARE WELCOME TO PEEL THEM IF YOU PREFER.

WE USE WHAT WE HAVE
EST 2022

CHAPTER FOUR

CASSEROLES & RICE DISHES

I'm here to show you that not every casserole is built on a can of condensed soup, and rice isn't just a side dish. The recipes in this chapter are just as dependable as the classics we grew up with, but have more variety (because my family doesn't want to eat the same thing over and over). Think blank canvases to help reuse those leftovers, dump-and-go dishes for when you only have 5 minutes to prep, and even special recipes to help you impress your guests on a budget.

WOW! CHICKEN CACCIATORE

SERVES 6

2 tablespoons neutral oil

½ cup (60 g) all-purpose flour

2 teaspoons salt

1 teaspoon pepper

1 whole chicken, cut into 8 pieces, or 2 to 3 pounds (1 to 1.5 kg) bone-in, skin-on chicken pieces

1 medium onion, cut into 1-inch (2.5 cm) pieces

1 bell pepper (any color), cut into 1-inch (2.5 cm) pieces

8 ounces (227 g) white mushrooms, cut into 1-inch (2.5 cm) pieces

2 medium carrots, peeled and sliced ¼ inch (6 mm) thick

3 garlic cloves, minced

¼ cup tomato paste

1 tablespoon Italian seasoning

½ cup (125 mL) chicken broth

1 (16-ounce/960 g) can diced tomatoes

¼ cup pitted green olives, chopped (optional)

2 teaspoons balsamic vinegar

1 teaspoon sugar

WHY: COOKING TOMATO PASTE GIVES IT A RICH DEPTH OF FLAVOR (IF YOU'VE EVER HAD A FLAT, MILD TOMATO SAUCE–BASED DISH, THIS IS PROBABLY THE STEP THAT GOT MISSED).

My mother-in-law requests my chicken cacciatore on her birthday almost every year. It's the first "big girl" dinner I learned to make while in university. If you want to impress your friends and family on a budget, this is the recipe—bone-in chicken cuts are some of the cheapest meat options out there, and when prepared correctly can still feel super special. Serve over rice or with a side of crusty bread.

1. Preheat the oven to 375°F (190°C). Coat a 9 × 13-inch baking dish with nonstick cooking spray.
2. Heat the oil in a Dutch oven or other large, heavy-bottomed pot over medium-high heat.
3. In a shallow bowl, mix together the flour, salt, and pepper. Pat the chicken pieces dry, then dredge in the seasoned flour. Set aside the remaining seasoned flour for later. Gently place the chicken pieces skin-side down in the hot oil. Cook for 2 to 3 minutes, then use tongs to flip the pieces and cook until browned on the other side, another 2 to 3 minutes. Transfer the browned chicken to the prepared baking dish.
4. Add the onion, bell pepper, mushrooms, and carrots to the same pot and sauté for a few minutes until they start to soften, then add the garlic and cook for another few minutes. Stir in 2 tablespoons of the reserved seasoned flour. Add the tomato paste and Italian seasoning and cook for about 3 minutes, until the tomato paste starts to brown.
5. Add the broth, tomatoes with their juice, olives (if using), vinegar, and sugar and stir to incorporate.
6. Pour the vegetable and sauce mixture over the chicken in the baking dish. Bake for 40 to 50 minutes, or until a meat thermometer inserted near the bone reads at least 165°F (74°C). Serve.

continues

ALTERNATIVE METHOD

For a weeknight version, you can make this recipe in the slow cooker. First, make sure you remove the spine from the chicken breasts as the cartilage tends to melt and the spine bits end up all through the dish. Omit the flour and chicken broth (you won't want the extra liquid if you aren't adding the thickener). Don't sauté anything (having to cook before slow cooking is one of my kitchen pet peeves!)—just layer everything over the chicken. Cover and cook on high for 4 hours or on low for 8 hours (but check it sooner as slow cooker temperatures vary by size and model).

USE WHAT YOU HAVE

INGREDIENT	TRY THIS INSTEAD:
Bone-in chicken	Bone-in pork chops
Diced tomatoes	Crushed tomatoes, stewed tomatoes
Balsamic vinegar + sugar	Dry red wine
Chicken broth	Water + bouillon

SWEET POTATO & LENTIL SHEPHERD'S PIE

SERVES 6 TO 8

MASHED POTATOES

4 medium sweet potatoes, peeled and cubed

6 medium russet or any white-fleshed potatoes, peeled and cubed

⅓ cup (75 g) butter

½ cup (125 mL) milk

½ teaspoon salt

LENTIL FILLING

1 tablespoon neutral oil

5 mushrooms, finely chopped

½ medium onion, finely chopped

1 medium carrot, peeled and finely chopped

1 (19-ounce/540 g) can brown lentils, rinsed and drained, *or* 2 cups (400 g) cooked brown lentils

1 cup (150 g) frozen corn kernels

½ cup (75 g) frozen peas

3 tablespoons all-purpose flour

2 teaspoons garlic powder

3 teaspoons onion powder

1 teaspoon dried oregano

1 teaspoon dried thyme

¼ teaspoon salt

¼ teaspoon pepper

2 teaspoons balsamic vinegar

1 (6-ounce/170 g) can tomato paste

1 teaspoon sugar

2 cups (500 mL) beef broth

2 cups (200 g) shredded cheddar cheese

These days even ground beef can be expensive. Brown lentils are a cost-effective swap, but not everyone is so easy to convince. I do find some recipes, like shepherd's pie, lend themselves more easily to the switch. I often look back at videos of my son feeding himself this dish as a baby—he would make an adorable "mumumum" sound with every bite. And yes, I know, shepherd's pie uses lamb, so this is technically cottage pie, but I'm not changing the name. ;)

---

1. Preheat the oven to 350°F (175°C).
2. Put all the potatoes in a large pot, cover with cold water, and lightly salt. Bring to a boil and cook until the potatoes are easily pierced with a fork, about 15 minutes. Drain the potatoes and return them to the pot. Mash in the butter, milk, and salt until smooth. Taste and adjust seasoning as desired.
3. Meanwhile, heat the oil in a large oven-safe skillet over medium heat. Add the mushrooms, onion, and carrot and sauté until softened, about 5 minutes. Add the lentils, corn, and peas and sauté for another few minutes. Mix in the flour to coat, then add the garlic powder, onion powder, oregano, thyme, salt, pepper, vinegar, and tomato paste. Mix well and sauté for about 2 minutes to cook the flour, deepen the tomato paste flavor, and cook off the acidity in the vinegar. Add the sugar and broth and bring to a light boil, then reduce the heat to a simmer and cook for 10 minutes.

WHY: STARTING POTATOES IN COLD WATER COOKS THEM EVENLY ALL THE WAY THROUGH. WHEN YOU PUT THEM INTO ALREADY BOILING WATER, THE OUTSIDE COOKS FASTER (WHICH IS GREAT FOR SMASHED POTATOES).

continues

4. Remove the pan from the heat and top with the mashed potatoes and shredded cheese. Transfer to the oven and bake for 15 minutes. If the cheese browns before the cook time is up, lightly cover with aluminum foil to prevent burning. Let stand for 5 minutes before serving.

USE WHAT YOU HAVE

INGREDIENT	TRY THIS INSTEAD:
Sweet potatoes	Any potatoes you have on hand
Brown lentils	2 pounds (900 g) ground beef or ground chicken
2 teaspoons balsamic vinegar + 1 teaspoon sugar	1 teaspoon apple cider vinegar + 1 teaspoon brown sugar (If you're removing the depth of flavor of the balsamic, put it back in with the brown sugar)
Tomato paste + beef broth	2 cups (500 mL) tomato sauce + 2 teaspoons beef bouillon or vegetable bouillon
Cheese	Can be omitted if dairy-free, but we love it!

RED LENTIL LASAGNA

SERVES 6

1 tablespoon neutral oil
1 medium onion, chopped
2 celery ribs, chopped
1 large carrot, peeled and chopped
3 garlic cloves, minced
1 (6-ounce/170 g) can tomato paste
2 teaspoons Italian seasoning
½ teaspoon salt
¼ teaspoon pepper
1 (28-ounce/794 g) can crushed tomatoes
2 teaspoons sugar
1 cup (200 g) red lentils
2 cups (500 mL) chicken broth
2 cups (500 g) cottage cheese
1 large egg
2 cups (200 g) shredded mozzarella cheese, divided
12 traditional lasagna noodles, uncooked
1 cup (100 g) shredded Italian blend cheese

Lasagna is one of those meals I used to avoid because of all the steps, until I learned that you don't have to pre-boil the noodles if you add a bit more liquid and cook time. This recipe uses regular lasagna noodles (*not* no-boil) and you can put them straight from the box into the casserole dish. Red lentil Bolognese is a pretty common dish, but we eat enough spaghetti as it is so this recipe is an easy way to switch it up from your standard tomato-based pasta. Bonus: Red lentils are pennies on the dollar to ground beef.

1. Preheat the oven to 375°F (190°C). Grease a 9 × 13 -inch baking dish with nonstick cooking spray.
2. Heat the oil in a large skillet over medium heat. Add the onion, celery, and carrot and sauté until they begin to soften, about 5 minutes. Add the garlic and sauté for another minute, then add the tomato paste, Italian seasoning, salt, and pepper. Cook for 2 to 3 minutes to deepen the flavors, then add the crushed tomatoes, sugar, lentils, and broth. Simmer for 15 minutes, or until the lentils soften.
3. Meanwhile, mix together the cottage cheese, eggs, and 1 cup (100 g) of the mozzarella in a bowl.
4. Spoon some of the sauce into the prepared baking dish to coat the bottom, then layer on 4 of the uncooked noodles, one-third of the cottage cheese mixture, and one-third of the remaining sauce. Repeat to make two more layers. Top with the Italian blend cheese and remaining 1 cup (100 g) mozzarella and loosely cover the dish with aluminum foil.
5. Bake for 40 minutes, then remove the foil and continue baking for another 10 minutes, until all the liquid is absorbed, the noodles are cooked through, and the cheese is melted and golden. Let stand for 10 minutes before cutting and serving.

USE WHAT YOU HAVE

INGREDIENT	TRY THIS INSTEAD:
Red lentils	Ground beef
Cottage cheese	Ricotta cheese, or omit the eggs and layer in the Italian cheese blend
Crushed tomatoes	Diced tomatoes or tomato sauce
Italian cheese blend	Shredded cheese of choice, preferably not more mozzarella for variety, but if that's all you have it's OK

BTW . . . I DO MEAN TO USE REGULAR LASAGNA NOODLES, NOT THE NO-COOK KIND. THERE'S ENOUGH LIQUID TO SOFTEN THEM UP AS THEY COOK.

WHITE BEAN SCALLOPED POTATOES

SERVES 4 TO 6

1 (19-ounce/540 g) can white kidney beans (cannellini), rinsed and drained

1½ cups (375 mL) milk

1 teaspoon veggie bouillon

¼ teaspoon dried thyme

5 medium white-fleshed potatoes of choice, scrubbed and thinly sliced

2 small zucchini, thinly sliced

1 medium onion, thinly sliced

3 cups (300 g) shredded Gouda cheese

Salt and pepper

Ketchup, for serving

I'm going to be straight with you: At this point I'm just trying to see where I can hide beans and get away with it. And get away I did with this scalloped-meets-gratin casserole because my oldest daughter, who *always* can detect the beans, did not. Beans are a cheap source of protein and fiber and they turn this typical side dish into a whole meal casserole. Serve with ketchup because, well, it's potatoes.

QUICK TIP: I use the slicing attachment on my rotary grater to save time and slice everything super thin.

1. Preheat the oven to 400°F (200°C). Grease a 9 × 13-inch casserole dish with nonstick cooking spray.
2. Combine the beans, milk, and bouillon in a blender and blend until smooth. Stir in the thyme.
3. Layer half of the potatoes, zucchini, and onion in the prepared casserole dish. Sprinkle with half of the cheese. Season lightly with salt and pepper, then pour half of the bean sauce over the vegetable layer. Repeat the vegetable, cheese, and sauce layers, but do not add more salt and pepper.
4. Cover tightly with aluminum foil and bake for 40 minutes, then remove the foil and bake for another 20 minutes. Let sit for at least 10 minutes before serving for the casserole to set up.

WHY: THE TOP LAYER WILL END UP DRYING OUT LATER, AND THE BOUILLON IN THE SAUCE WILL BE SALTY ENOUGH.

BTW . . . NO NEED TO PEEL THE POTATOES HERE, UNLESS YOU PREFER THEM THAT WAY.

USE WHAT YOU HAVE

INGREDIENT	TRY THIS INSTEAD:
Zucchini	Shredded carrots, peas, corn
Gouda cheese	Italian blend, or cheddar + mozzarella
Veggie bouillon	Chicken bouillon (avoid using beef as its flavor is deeper, plus your dish will turn brownish) OR Salt + garlic powder + onion powder

CREAM OF ANYTHING CASSEROLE

SERVES 6

1½ cups (300 g) uncooked white rice

2 cups (300 g) chopped cooked chicken or leftover rotisserie chicken

2 cups (300 g) fresh or frozen chopped vegetables of choice

½ cup (125 mL) cottage cheese

1 (10-ounce/284 mL) can condensed cream of chicken soup or cream soup of choice

1 can water

2 teaspoons chicken bouillon

1 teaspoon onion powder

1 teaspoon garlic powder

1 teaspoon dried parsley

½ teaspoon pepper

1 cup (100 g) shredded cheddar cheese

1 cup fried onions (optional)

This recipe is one of my husband's favorites and was originally in my leftover transformation repertoire, but you can also make this casserole with canned chicken or tuna or chickpeas, or omit the protein and just increase the veggies (use veggie bouillon and cream of vegetable soup for a vegetarian version). I like to use broccoli, green beans, and corn, but you can use any fresh or frozen veggies you like or have on hand. Bonus: It takes only about 3 minutes to prep.

1. Preheat the oven to 400°F (200°C). Grease a 9 × 13-inch casserole dish with nonstick cooking spray.
2. Combine the rice, chicken, vegetables, cottage cheese, soup, water, bouillon, onion powder, garlic powder, parsley, and pepper in the prepared casserole dish and mix well. Tightly cover with aluminum foil and bake for 50 minutes. Remove the foil, top with the shredded cheese and fried onions (if using) and return to the oven for another 5 to 10 minutes, or until the rice is cooked and the cheese has melted. Let sit for 10 minutes before serving.

WEEKNIGHT BURRITO CASSEROLE

MAKES 5 BURRITOS

¾ cup (150 g) white rice

2 small sweet potatoes

1 tablespoon neutral oil

1 medium onion, diced

2 garlic cloves, minced

1 (19-ounce/540 g) can black beans, rinsed and drained

2 cups (300 g) frozen corn kernels

1 tablespoon chili powder

1 teaspoon ground cumin

1 teaspoon dried oregano

½ teaspoon salt

¼ teaspoon pepper

5 large flour tortillas

1¼ cup (300 g) salsa, divided

2 cups (200 g) shredded cheddar cheese

Sour cream or Greek yogurt, for serving

Sliced green onions, for serving

In 2019, I went full vegan and took my whole family on a journey they never asked for (more on that on page 12). Burrito casserole was probably the meal my husband appreciated the most, and it's super easy to throw together. I now make it using real dairy as we obviously no longer follow a plant-based diet. Top with sour cream or Greek yogurt and serve on a plate with a fork and knife.

1. Preheat the oven to 350°F (175°C). Grease a 9 × 13-inch casserole dish with nonstick cooking spray.
2. Cook the rice according to the package directions.
3. Meanwhile, pierce the sweet potatoes all over with a fork. Microwave on a plate until soft enough to easily pierce with a fork, about 10 minutes. Once cool enough to handle, peel the sweet potatoes and mash the flesh with a fork.
4. Heat the oil in a large skillet over medium heat. Add the onion and sauté until it begins to soften, about 5 minutes. Add the garlic and sauté for another minute. Stir in the beans, corn, chili powder, cumin, oregano, salt, and pepper and cook for a few minutes longer.
5. Lay out the tortillas and smear an even portion of the mashed sweet potatoes down the center of each tortilla. Spoon even portions of the bean and corn mixture on top of the potatoes. Mix together the cooked rice and ½ cup (125 g) of the salsa, then divide among the tortillas. Sprinkle cheese on each tortilla, using about a cup of it.
6. Wrap up the burritos and line them up in the prepared casserole dish. Top with the remaining ¾ cup (175 g) salsa and remaining 1 cup (100 g) cheese. Bake until the burritos are warmed through and crisp and the cheese is melted, about 15 minutes. Serve topped with sour cream or Greek yogurt and sliced green onions.

ROAST DINNER POT PIE

VARIES

This simple pot pie–style casserole repurposes leftovers from a roast dinner. It's a formula, not a fixed recipe, so I've made a table with recommended pairings, although you can mix and match however you like. The prep time on this is around 5 minutes, so it's perfect for a busy weeknight. If using mashed potatoes, you can prepare the casserole ahead and freeze it to pull out at a later date, which I often do when my family isn't in the mood for those leftovers yet.

COOKED LEFTOVERS	GRAVY	SEASONING	TOPPING
Chicken	Condensed cream of chicken soup	Poultry seasoning	Puff pastry
Pork	Condensed cream of mushroom soup	Dried rosemary	Stuffing mix
Roast beef	Brown gravy	Dried thyme	Mashed potatoes
Roasted vegetables	Mushroom gravy	Dried oregano, pepper	Biscuit dough

1. Preheat the oven according to the package directions for your chosen topping. For mashed potatoes you can use 375°F (190°C). Spray a casserole dish with nonstick cooking spray.
2. Chop all the meat/vegetables to approximately the same size. Combine the meat/vegetables, gravy, and seasoning in the prepared casserole dish. Top with your choice of topping and bake according to the package directions, or until a meat thermometer inserted reaches 165°F (74°C). Let cool for 5 minutes before serving.

WHY: EVEN SIZES WILL REHEAT MORE EVENLY.

BTW . . . DISH SIZE AND COOK TIME DEPEND ON HOW MANY LEFTOVERS YOU HAVE. KEEP AN EYE ON THE TOPPING AND LOOSELY COVER WITH ALUMINUM FOIL ONCE IT LOOKS BROWNED TO AVOID BURNING.

TURKEY & RICE STUFFED SQUASH

SERVES 4

1 buttercup or acorn squash

½ teaspoon salt, plus more for the squash

1 tablespoon olive oil or neutral oil

1 pound (454 g) ground turkey

½ medium onion, finely chopped

1 celery rib, finely chopped

3 garlic cloves, minced

¾ cup (150 g) long-grain white and wild rice mix

1½ cups (375 mL) chicken broth

2 teaspoons garlic powder

1 teaspoons onion powder

1 teaspoon ground sage

¼ teaspoon pepper

1 cup (100 g) shredded mozzarella cheese

WHY: YOU NEED A FEW HOLES TO LET THE STEAM ESCAPE.

Anything stuffed looks fancy to me, so this is a great recipe to pull out when you're having guests. Plus, individual components for this meal can be prepared ahead, then assembled before cooking (the cooking time will increase if the components are refrigerated). This can also be made deconstructed (see Tip below). Look for a round squash, not butternut. You need something that will form a bowl once you scoop out the seeds.

1. Preheat the oven to 400°F (200°C). Line a rimmed baking sheet with aluminum foil.
2. Cut the squash in half and scoop out the seeds. Lightly salt the squash flesh and place the halves cut side down on the lined baking sheet. Carefully poke some holes in the squash skin with a knife. Bake until soft enough to easily puncture with a fork, about 30 minutes.
3. Meanwhile, heat the oil in a large skillet over medium heat. Add the ground turkey and sauté, stirring often, until it's mostly browned, about 8 minutes. Add the onion, celery, and garlic and cook until the onion is translucent and the meat is cooked through, about 5 more minutes. Add the rice, broth, garlic powder, onion powder, sage, salt, and pepper. Cover and cook according to the time on the rice package or until all the liquid is absorbed and the rice is tender.
4. Remove the squash halves from the oven, flip them over, and fill with equal amounts of the rice mixture. Top with the cheese and return to the oven for 10 more minutes, or until the cheese is melted and lightly browned. Let cool for 5 to 10 minutes before carefully cutting each squash half in half again to make 4 servings.

continues

ALTERNATIVE METHOD

For a deconstructed dish, peel and cube the squash into bite-size pieces and lightly coat in oil, salt, and pepper. Roast at 400°F (200°C) until a fork easily pierces through and the squash begins to caramelize, about 40 minutes, flipping halfway. Follow step 3 as above and serve everything together in bowls.

USE WHAT YOU HAVE

INGREDIENT	TRY THIS INSTEAD:
Ground turkey	Ground chicken or mild sausage removed from its casings (use half the seasonings); avoid ground beef as it is a bit too rich for this recipe
Ground sage	Poultry seasoning, dried rosemary, dried thyme, dried oregano
Wild rice	Basmati rice or more long-grain white rice; avoid sticky rice such as jasmine
Squash	Sweet potato (in the deconstructed version), large zucchini (think zucchini boats); if you go the route of stuffed bell pepper, choose a sweeter color like yellow or red

COZY RICE & BEANS WITH PORK BELLY

SERVES 4 TO 6

1½ cups (300 g) white rice

2 teaspoons vegetable bouillon

1 to 2 tablespoons neutral oil

2 ripe plantains (see Tip), peeled and sliced

Salt and pepper

8 pork belly strips (12 ounces/375 g)

¼ cup (60 mL) barbecue sauce

1 (14-ounce/398 g) can homestyle baked beans

1 teaspoon dried oregano

½ teaspoon smoked paprika

½ teaspoon garlic powder

½ teaspoon onion powder

Thinly sliced green onions and diced avocado, to serve

Sometimes I joke that I was born in the wrong climate because nothing comforts me more than rice, beans, and a bit of meat. This dish is not authentic but is inspired by Caribbean and South American cuisine, and I hope you love it as much as I do.

Pork belly strips are thick uncured bacon-looking pieces. It may not be the absolute cheapest cut by weight, but my store usually sells very small packages, and a little goes a long way. If you can't find it, you can cut a larger piece of pork belly yourself or find pork chops with a nice layer of fat along one edge—that's where the magic happens. Cut that into strips, keeping some fat on each piece.

---

1. Cook the rice, including the bouillon, according to the package directions.
2. Meanwhile, heat the oil in a large, heavy-bottomed skillet (I use cast iron) over medium heat. Add the plantain slices in a single layer and cook for about 3 minutes, until browned and soft, then flip, lightly season with salt and pepper, and cook for another 3 minutes, or until soft. Press down on the plantains with a spatula to flatten slightly. Transfer the plantains to a plate.
3. Add the pork belly strips to the oil remaining in the pan and cook over medium heat until the edges are seared and the fat is rendered, about 6 minutes. flipping once and brushing with the barbecue sauce on both sides. The pork should reach an internal temperature of at least 145°F (63°C), but I usually stick to the standard 165°F (74°C). Transfer to a cutting board and let rest for 5 minutes before slicing.
4. Meanwhile, combine the beans, oregano, smoked paprika, garlic powder, and onion powder in a small saucepan. Cook over medium heat until heated through, about 5 minutes.
5. Serve the rice in bowls topped with the plantains, pork, and beans, and garnished with thinly sliced green onions and diced avocado.

BTW . . . HOW DO YOU PICK A RIPE PLANTAIN? LOOK FOR YELLOW PEELS WITH LOTS OF BROWN. IF YOU CAN ONLY FIND GREEN ONES, YOU'LL WANT TO LET THEM RIPEN FOR A FEW DAYS FIRST AS THEY WILL BE VERY HARD TO PEEL. SIMILAR TO BANANAS, PLANTAINS GET SWEETER WHEN THEY RIPEN, BUT A RIPE PLANTAIN IS PROBABLY ONLY ABOUT AS SWEET AS A SWEET POTATO.

DUMP & BAKE VEGGIE RICE

SERVES 4 TO 6

1 cup (200 g) parboiled rice

3 cups (450 g) finely chopped fresh or frozen vegetables of choice

2 cups (300 g) chopped rotisserie or leftover cooked chicken (optional, but recommended)

1 (1-ounce/28 g) packet onion soup mix

1 teaspoon garlic powder

¼ teaspoon pepper

2 cups water

1 tablespoon soy sauce

2 tablespoons butter, cut into cubes

If there's one thing I love, it's a good dump meal. This baked rice with chicken and vegetables was my first-ever viral recipe and for good reason: It's a complete meal in under 5 minutes of prep and is very kid-friendly. Feel free to clean out your vegetable drawer on this one and use whatever you have—just make sure to chop everything tiny so it all cooks through. My family also likes the frozen mixed veggie blend with green beans, carrots, peas, and corn.

1. Preheat the oven to 400°F (200°C). Grease a 9 × 13-inch casserole dish with nonstick cooking spray.
2. Combine the rice, vegetables, chicken (if using), onion soup mix, garlic powder, pepper, water, and soy sauce in the prepared casserole dish. Distribute the butter cubes on top. Cover the dish with aluminum foil and bake for 40 to 50 minutes, until most of the liquid has been absorbed.
3. Uncover, stir everything together, and let sit for 10 minutes before serving.

USE WHAT YOU HAVE

INGREDIENT	TRY THIS INSTEAD:
Parboiled rice, aka converted rice (rice that has been partially cooked but is sold dried)	Basmati rice, long-grain white rice; cook times will vary.
Onion soup mix	1½ tablespoons beef bouillon + 1 tablespoon onion powder

DIRTY-ISH RICE

SERVES 4 TO 6

1 tablespoon neutral oil

1 pound (454 g) ground beef

½ medium onion, finely chopped

1 celery rib, finely chopped

1 carrot, peeled and finely chopped

½ green bell pepper, finely chopped

3 garlic cloves, minced

2 teaspoons paprika

2 teaspoons dried parsley

1 teaspoon dried oregano

1 teaspoon onion powder

1 teaspoon garlic powder

1 teaspoon ground cumin

¼ teaspoon pepper

1 (19-ounce/540 g) can brown lentils, rinsed and drained, *or* 2 cups (400 g) cooked brown lentils

1 tablespoon chicken bouillon

1½ cups (300 g) parboiled rice

1½ cups (375 mL) water

1 tablespoon butter

WHY: IF THE LIQUID IS TOO THICK, IT CANNOT BUILD ENOUGH STEAM TO COME TO PRESSURE. BUT THE MACHINE WILL KEEP HEATING WHILE IT TRIES, CAUSING THE FOOD ON THE BOTTOM TO BURN.

My kids think cumin is spicy, but somehow this delicious-but-not-authentic take on dirty rice goes over well every time. When I got my electric pressure cooker, I went on a rice kick because it cooks up better than I've ever been able to manage on the stovetop (but don't worry if you don't have one because I still included stovetop instructions). I use brown lentils to "stretch" the beef, so you still get the flavor, plus extra fiber, at a lower cost.

---

1. Heat the oil in an electric pressure cooker on the Sauté function. Add the beef and sauté until browned, breaking up the meat with a spatula, about 7 minutes. If the beef has a lot of grease, you can make a well in the middle of the pot and soak some up with a paper towel, then add the onion, celery, bell pepper, and garlic. Sauté for about 5 minutes, until the onion and celery soften. Add the paprika, parsley, oregano, onion powder, garlic powder, cumin, and pepper and sauté for 1 minute to bring out their flavors.
2. Add the lentils, bouillon, rice, water, and butter but *do not stir* as this can cause the pressure cooker to give you a burn notice. Set the cooker to high for 5 minutes, then naturally release for 10 minutes and vent. Open the lid, taste, and adjust the salt and pepper if desired. Serve.

ALTERNATIVE METHOD

To make this on the stovetop, follow step 1 in a large saucepan over medium heat. In step 2, add 3 cups (750 mL) water instead of 1½ cups and bring to a boil, then reduce the heat, cover, and cook according to the rice package directions (usually 15 to 20 minutes).

SHEET PAN GRIDDLE PANCAKES

SERVES 6

6 breakfast sausages

4 large eggs, divided

1 cup (250 mL) milk, plus more for the eggs

1½ cups (180 g) all-purpose flour

¼ cup (53 g) brown sugar

1 tablespoon baking powder

¼ teaspoon salt

1 teaspoon vanilla extract

3 slices processed (aka American) cheese, cut into bite-size pieces

2 tablespoons maple syrup or table syrup

I love the golden arches griddle sandwich, and this sheet pan version at home satisfies in the same way—sweet and savory, pillowy goodness. Feel free to mix up the toppings to suit your preferences or to use up things like leftover boiled eggs and extra deli ham.

1. Preheat the oven to 375°F (190°C). Line a rimmed baking sheet with parchment paper and lightly spray with nonstick cooking spray.
2. Cook the sausages according to the package directions. (I pan-fry mine, covered, until they reach an internal temperature of 165°F/74°C.) Beat 3 of the eggs with a few splashes of milk. Once the sausages are cooked, transfer them to a cutting board and cut into bite-size pieces. Add the eggs to the same pan and scramble until just cooked, about 5 minutes, then remove the pan from the heat.
3. Mix together the flour, brown sugar, baking powder, salt, milk, and vanilla. Spread the batter mixture on the prepared baking sheet. Distribute the cheese, sausage, and scrambled eggs evenly across the batter.
4. Bake for 20 to 25 minutes, until the center of the pancake is set but not dry, then immediately drizzle the maple syrup over the top. Let the syrup sink into the pancake for a few minutes before removing from the pan and slicing. **HOT TIP: If making ahead, refrigerate for up to 3 days and reheat slices on a paper towel in the microwave for 15 to 30 seconds.** The paper towel will absorb extra moisture so the pancake doesn't get soggy.

USE WHAT YOU HAVE

TRY MAKING A SWEET VERSION WITH THESE TOPPINGS:
Thinly sliced apple + ground cinnamon
Overripe mashed banana (mixed into batter) + chocolate chips
Blueberries or mixed berries

CROISSANT CASSEROLE

SERVES 4 TO 6

6 large croissants, cut crosswise into 2-inch pieces

9 large eggs

½ cup (125 mL) milk

1 tablespoon garlic powder

1 tablespoon onion powder

½ teaspoon salt

¼ teaspoon pepper

4 ounces (125 g) sliced pastrami, cut into 1-inch strips

6 slices Swiss cheese, quartered

1 tablespoon everything bagel seasoning, divided

1 avocado, peeled, pitted, and chopped

Years ago, I had a breakfast cookbook from HomeSense that had a pastrami, Swiss cheese, and avocado egg sandwich in it, and I still love that flavor combination. So, it was a no-brainer for me when croissant casseroles were going viral to make one with those ingredients, and I have to say, I was so, so right.

1. Preheat the oven to 375°F (190°C). Grease a 9 × 9-inch casserole dish with nonstick cooking spray.
2. Lay out the croissant pieces in the prepared casserole dish. Beat the eggs with the milk, garlic powder, onion powder, salt, and pepper. Pour the mixture over the croissants and toss to coat. Stuff the pastrami strips and Swiss cheese pieces between the croissant pieces, then sprinkle with ½ tablespoon of the everything bagel seasoning.
3. Bake the casserole for 15 to 20 minutes, until the eggs set up. Check the sides and middle as you may see some wetness around the cheese from its oils, where the eggs are actually fully set. Let cool and set up for 5 minutes.
4. Scatter the avocado and remaining ½ tablespoon everything bagel seasoning over the casserole. Slice into squares to serve.

MORE FLAVOR COMBOS TO TRY

SAVORY	SWEET (SWAP THE SEASONINGS FOR 1 TABLESPOON BROWN SUGAR + 2 TEASPOONS GROUND CINNAMON)
Bacon or ham + cheddar	Frozen blueberries + cream cheese
Leftover steak fajita strips + roasted bell peppers and onions	Frozen strawberry slices + chocolate chips

CHAPTER FIVE

SANDWICHES & WRAPS

You don't need a big budget or fancy ingredients for supper—you just need bread. Our '90s moms knew this because every meal came with a slice of buttered white. Back then it seemed like sandwiches were strictly for lunch, but there's so much you can do to make them feel like dinner, and this chapter has recipes for whatever you've got on hand—whether it's piling those veggies high or using unconventional fillings like lentils. Now go make yourself a delicious sandwich. ;)

SNEAKY SLOPPY JOES

MAKES 8 SANDWICHES

- 1 tablespoon neutral oil
- 1 pound (454 g) ground beef
- ½ medium onion, finely chopped
- ½ green bell pepper, finely chopped
- 1 (6-ounce/170 g) can tomato paste
- 1 (19-ounce/540 g) can brown lentils, rinsed and drained, *or* 2 cups (400 g) cooked brown lentils
- 2 teaspoons garlic powder
- 2 teaspoons dried oregano
- ½ teaspoon salt
- ½ teaspoon pepper
- 2 teaspoons beef bouillon
- ½ cup water
- ½ cup ketchup
- 1 tablespoon yellow mustard
- 2 tablespoons brown sugar
- 1 tablespoon Worcestershire sauce
- 8 hamburger buns
- 8 processed (aka American) or cheddar cheese slices

✳ WITH SLOPPY JOES, YOU'RE TRYING TO MAKE A TOMATO-HEAVY SAUCE THAT BALANCES ACIDITY (VINEGAR IN KETCHUP, MUSTARD), SWEETNESS (SUGAR IN KETCHUP, BROWN SUGAR, WORCESTERSHIRE), AND SALTINESS (BOUILLON, WORCESTERSHIRE). IF YOU TAKE ONE OUT, YOU'LL WANT TO REPLACE IT ELSEWHERE.

I love the challenge of sneaking things into recipes to make them more affordable *and* healthier. Lentils are a great way to stretch ground beef—the ultimate budget hack IMO. The rich tomato BBQ sauce makes them blend right in—but you can use all beef or all lentils if you prefer. Serve these alongside veggies and dip to round out the meal.

1. Heat the oil in a large skillet over medium heat. Add the ground beef and sauté, using a spatula to break the meat into crumbles, until mostly browned, about 7 minutes. If the beef has a lot of grease, you can make a well in the middle of the pan and soak some up with a paper towel. Add the onion and bell pepper and cook until the onion begins to soften, about 5 minutes. Add the tomato paste and sauté for a minute to deepen the flavor. Add the lentils, garlic powder, oregano, salt, pepper, bouillon, water, ketchup, mustard, brown sugar, and Worcestershire and mix well. Cover the pan, reduce the heat to simmer, and cook for about 15 minutes for the flavors to meld.
2. Meanwhile, toast the buns. Scoop a generous spoonful of sloppy joe mix onto the bottom halves of the buns, then top with a slice of cheese and the other half of the buns. Serve.

USE WHAT YOU HAVE

INGREDIENT	TRY THIS INSTEAD:
Beef + lentils	All beef, all lentils, or ground chicken
Ketchup	Tomato paste + sugar + vinegar
Worcestershire	Soy sauce + sugar
Brown sugar	White sugar + molasses

OVEN CHEESEBURGERS (AKA CHEESESTEAK SLIDERS)

MAKES 12 MINI SLIDERS

1 tablespoon neutral oil
1 pound (454 g) ground beef
1 medium onions, sliced
½ green bell pepper, sliced
½ orange bell pepper, sliced
2 teaspoons garlic powder
2 teaspoons paprika
¾ teaspoon salt
½ teaspoon pepper
1 (12-pack) Hawaiian slider rolls, not separated
1 tablespoon mayonnaise
1 tablespoon yellow mustard
1 teaspoon hot sauce (optional)
2 cups (200 g) shredded mozzarella cheese
1 tablespoon butter, melted
Sea salt (optional)

BTW . . . I RECOMMEND SHREDDING YOUR OWN CHEESE IF POSSIBLE, AS PRESHREDDED CHEESE HAS A COATING THAT DOESN'T MELT AS WELL.

You call it gaslighting; I call it *mommy marketing*—either way I can get my kids to try pretty much anything—even bell peppers. Mommy marketing is really just naming things something your kids already like, and nobody is turning down a cheeseburger in my house! **QUICK TIP: Swap the fresh peppers and onions for frozen (no chopping required!).**

1. Preheat the oven to 350°F (175°C). Lightly grease a 9 × 13-inch casserole dish with nonstick cooking spray.
2. Heat the oil in a large, heavy-bottomed skillet over medium heat. Add the ground beef and cook until it begins to brown, about 7 minutes. If the beef has a lot of grease, you can make a well in the middle of the pan and soak some up with a paper towel. Add the onion and cook until the onion begins to soften and the beef is cooked, about 4 minutes. Add the bell pepper strips, garlic powder, paprika, salt, and pepper and cook until the peppers are softened, about 5 minutes.
3. Slice the whole package of Hawaiian rolls in half horizontally, trying your best to keep them attached so you have two large halves—that is, all the bottoms are connected and all the tops are connected.
4. Place the roll bottoms in the prepared casserole dish. Mix together the mayonnaise, mustard, and hot sauce (if using). Spread the sauce across the bottom buns, then cover evenly with the beef and vegetable mixture, sprinkle the shredded cheese over the beef, and top with the other half of the rolls.
5. Brush the tops of the rolls with the melted butter and lightly sprinkle with sea salt (if using). Bake for about 10 minutes, until the cheese melts and the buns are toasty but not burnt. **HOT TIP: If your buns are browning too quickly, lay a piece of aluminum foil over the top to prevent burning.** Cut along the bun lines and serve.

PULLED PORK GRILLED CHEESE

MAKES 4 LARGE OR 8 SMALL SANDWICHES

PULLED PORK

1 pound (454 g) pork tenderloin

2 tablespoons brown sugar

1 teaspoon garlic powder

1 teaspoon onion powder

1 teaspoon paprika

1 teaspoon chili powder

¼ teaspoon dried thyme

¼ teaspoon salt, plus more to taste

⅛ teaspoon pepper, plus more to taste

2 teaspoons neutral oil

2 teaspoons yellow mustard

1 teaspoon Worcestershire sauce

1 teaspoon apple cider vinegar

½ cup (125 mL) barbecue sauce, divided

1 medium yellow onion, thinly sliced

3 garlic cloves, minced

SANDWICHES

½ cup (125 mL) mayonnaise

1 teaspoon garlic powder

Salt

1 loaf hearty bread, such as sourdough or ciabatta, sliced

1 (14-ounce/400 g) block mild cheddar cheese, shredded

1 cup sliced sweet pickles

1 cup sliced dill pickles

When we went to Disney World, one of our favorite meals was the brisket grilled cheese sandwich at Woody's Lunch Box, so I had to make my own version. You don't need a ton of meat, so I use a small pork tenderloin. This cut can be tricky to cook and often turns out dry, but tossing it into the slow cooker and turning it into pulled pork ensures it's tender and juicy every time.

---

1. Grease a slow cooker insert with nonstick cooking spray and add the pork tenderloin. Mix together the brown sugar, garlic powder, onion powder, paprika, chili powder, thyme, salt, pepper, oil, mustard, Worcestershire, and vinegar in a small bowl. Coat the pork tenderloin with the mixture, then drizzle with ¼ cup (60 mL) of the barbecue sauce. Add the onion and garlic. Cover and cook on high for 2 to 4 hours or on low for 4 to 6 hours.

2. Turn off the slow cooker. Shred the cooked pork directly in the slow cooker, being careful not to touch the sides as it will be very hot. I like to use a potato masher, or you can use two forks. Mix in the remaining ¼ cup (60 mL) barbecue sauce and toss to coat.

3. Preheat a large, heavy skillet (I use cast iron) over medium heat.

4. Meanwhile, mix together the mayonnaise, garlic powder, and salt to taste. Lay the bread slices out and spread one side of each with a thin layer of the mayonnaise mixture. The mayonnaise side will be on the outside of the sandwich, so flip over half of the bread slices. Top each with a generous sprinkle of cheese. Layer with a few tablespoons of the pulled pork and a few slices of each pickle, then sprinkle with more cheese and top the sandwiches with the remaining bread slices, mayonnaise side up.

continues

WHY: THIS ALLOWS A BIT OF THE MOISTURE TO ESCAPE SO THE SANDWICHES DON'T BECOME SOGGY.

5. Gently lower the sandwiches into the heated pan. You will have to work in batches depending on your sandwich size and pan size. Cover the pan with a lid placed slightly offset or an inverted sheet pan. Cook for 3 to 5 minutes, then check that the bottoms got crisp and the cheese began to melt before flipping. **HOT TIP: Use tongs in one hand and a spatula in the other to make sure the sandwiches stay together as you flip them.** Cover the pan again and cook for another 3 to 5 minutes, until the cheese has fully melted and the other piece of bread is toasted. Let rest for a few minutes to firm up slightly before cutting and serving.

USE WHAT YOU HAVE

INGREDIENT	TRY THIS INSTEAD:
Pork tenderloin	Boneless pork chops, boneless chicken, or bone-in chicken or pork, but use up to double as bones account for a lot of the weight
Bread	Flour tortillas to make quesadillas
Pickles	Sliced onions added to slow cooker to caramelize
Mild cheddar	Mix of shredded cheeses

HIDDEN VEGGIE TUNA MELT BURGERS

MAKES 8 TUNA BURGERS

- 2 (6-ounce/170 g) cans tuna, drained
- 1 large carrot, peeled and shredded
- 2 cups (200 g) shredded sharp cheddar cheese
- 1 cup (100 g) shredded mozzarella cheese
- ¼ cup (60 mL) mayonnaise
- 2 teaspoons lemon juice (optional)
- 1 teaspoon onion powder
- 1 teaspoon garlic powder
- 1 teaspoon dried parsley
- ¼ teaspoon salt, plus more to taste
- ¼ teaspoon pepper
- 8 hamburger buns
- 1 tablespoon butter, melted (optional)
- Sea salt (optional)
- 1 tablespoon honey
- 1 tablespoon yellow mustard

To my kids' chagrin, I love sneaking veggies into their food. My best trick is to grate everything—Is it cheese? Is it carrot? Nobody knows! My husband loves tuna melts, so we make these all the time, but if you form them into burgers it feels a little more fun ;) **HOT TIP: Grating the carrot on a cheese grater helps it blend in with the cheese and cook quickly.**

1. Preheat the oven to 350°F (175°C).
2. In a large bowl, combine the tuna, carrot, 1 cup (100 g) of the cheddar cheese, the mozzarella, mayo, lemon juice (if using), onion powder, garlic powder, parsley, salt, and pepper and mix well. Form the tuna mixture into 8 equal patties. **HOT TIP: Use an ice cream scoop to divide the mixture into 8 equal portions, then press with your hands into patties.**
3. Lay out the bottom halves of the buns cut side up on a rimmed baking sheet and toast in the oven for 3 to 5 minutes, checking that they don't burn. If you like, transfer the bottom buns to a plate, then paint the uncut side of the top buns with melted butter, sprinkle lightly with sea salt, and toast in the oven for another 3 minutes.
4. Meanwhile, mix together the honey and mustard in a small bowl. Once the buns are toasted, transfer the tops to a plate. Spread the honey mustard on the bun bottoms, then place a tuna patty on each. Sprinkle with the remaining 1 cup (100 g) cheddar cheese, then place in the oven for 10 to 15 minutes, until the tuna is heated through and the cheese is melted. Top each tuna burger with a bun top and serve while still warm.

ALTERNATIVE METHOD

Make these entirely on the stovetop by pan-toasting the buns in a bit of melted butter (skip painting the tops with melted butter if using this method). Once the buns are toasted, cook the patties in the same pan for a few minutes, just until heated through, then flip and sprinkle on the cheese. Cover the pan to melt the cheese, then assemble the burgers—add lettuce if you like!

LEFTOVER BUNDLES

MAKES 8 BUNDLES

- 2 (8-count) tubes crescent roll dough
- 2 cups (300 g) chopped cooked chicken
- 2 cups (300 g) chopped fresh or frozen vegetables of choice
- 1½ cups (150 g) shredded cheddar cheese
- ¼ cup (60 mL) mayonnaise
- 2 teaspoons onion powder
- 2 teaspoons garlic powder
- 2 teaspoons dried parsley
- 1 teaspoon paprika
- ½ teaspoon salt
- ¼ teaspoon pepper

This is the recipe that turned me from girlfriend to wife! One of my roommates introduced me to chicken bundles in university, and I made my own version for Andrew very early on in our relationship. That same night he told me he loved me, so I guess sometimes it's right what they say about the way to a man's heart! Use whatever veggies you have on hand; I like diced bell pepper, green onions, frozen corn, and a few diced cherry tomatoes, or try out other kinds of premade dough (cook time will vary).

1. Preheat the oven to 375°F (190°C). Line a rimmed baking sheet with parchment paper.
2. Unroll the crescent dough on the lined baking sheet. Separate each can of dough into 4 squares and pinch along the seam that connects them.
3. In a large bowl, combine the chicken, vegetables, cheese, mayo, onion powder, garlic powder, parsley, paprika, salt, and pepper and mix well. Spoon an equal amount (about ½ cup) onto each dough square.
4. Lift all 4 corners of each dough square together and pinch together, then pinch the edges together so it forms a fully closed pocket.
5. Bake until the bundles are golden brown, about 12 minutes. Let cool for 5 minutes before serving.

BTW . . . BASIL ADDS A WONDERFUL FLAVOR, BUT IF I'M USING WHAT I HAVE IT'S MORE LIKELY THAT I HAVE BABY SPINACH FOR THE "SOMETHING GREEN, SOMETHING FRESH" ELEMENT. FEEL FREE TO SPRINKLE SOME DRIED BASIL OVER THE CHEESE AND CALL IT A DAY.

DAD'S CHICKEN PARM SAMMIES

MAKES 4 SANDWICHES

GARLIC TOAST

8 slices Italian bread or other oval hearty bread

1 tablespoon olive oil

1 garlic clove, peeled and halved

CHICKEN

⅓ cup (40 g) Italian breadcrumbs

2 teaspoons dried parsley

2 teaspoons garlic powder

2 teaspoons onion powder

1 teaspoon salt

½ teaspoon pepper

2 large boneless, skinless chicken breasts, *or* 4 boneless, skinless chicken thighs (1 pound/454 g total)

2 to 4 tablespoons neutral oil

1 cup (250 mL) marinara sauce *or* 1 (8-ounce/227 g) can pizza sauce

4 ounces (115 g) fresh mozzarella, cut into 4 slices

½ cup (50 g) grated Parmesan cheese

Fresh basil leaves (optional)

My husband loves a good sandwich for supper. When I started making these years ago, it was frozen chicken burgers with canned pizza sauce and cheese on frozen garlic toast. While that version is still totally fine, the from-scratch version actually doesn't take any longer than the from-frozen one, and costs about the same. Alternatively, you could do this with eggplant slices (think eggplant parm). I like to serve a simple salad for an easy side (like *really* simple—think lettuce, cucumber, dressing—that's it).

1. Preheat the oven to 400°F (200°C). Line a rimmed baking sheet with parchment paper.
2. Lay out the bread slices on the lined baking sheet and drizzle with the olive oil. Toast the bread in the oven for about 5 minutes, until golden, then rub the cut sides of the garlic clove on the bread.
3. Mix the breadcrumbs, parsley, garlic powder, onion powder, salt, and pepper in a shallow bowl. Slice each chicken breast in half horizontally so you end up with 4 thin, flat cutlets. Coat the cutlets with the breadcrumb mixture.
4. Heat the oil in a large skillet over medium-high heat. I prefer shallow frying because it achieves a similar golden crust to deep frying but with less oil. Once the oil is hot, gently lower in the chicken cutlets to shallow-fry for 3 to 5 minutes per side, until the coating is browned and a meat thermometer inserted reaches 165°F (74°C). Transfer to a paper towel–lined plate to drain excess oil.
5. To assemble the sandwiches, spoon a bit of marinara sauce on half of the bread slices, then layer one chicken cutlet, more sauce, and some mozzarella and Parmesan on top. Place in the oven and bake until the mozzarella melts, about 7 minutes, then let cool for a few minutes before adding some basil leaves (if using) and topping with the remaining bread slices. Serve.

WHY: THIS WILL MICRO-GRATE GARLIC FLAVOR OVER THE BREAD DUE TO THE ROUGH TEXTURE OF THE TOAST.

WHY: IF THE BASIL GETS TOO HOT, IT WILL TURN BLACK.

MAC & CHEESE HOT DOGS

MAKES 8 HOT DOGS

1 (7.25-ounce/200 g) box macaroni and cheese, plus the required milk and butter

1 tablespoon yellow mustard (optional)

8 hot dogs

8 hot dog buns

Butter, for spreading on buns

1 cup shredded marble cheddar or Colby Jack cheese

Ketchup, for topping

1 cup potato chips, crushed

Hot dogs in mac 'n' cheese is a classic, so I thought I'd reverse it by putting the mac 'n' cheese in the hot dogs. It's a super fun twist—bonus points if you crush some chips on top for crunch. This is also a good recipe for leftover mac 'n' cheese or leftover grilled hot dogs.

1. Prepare the macaroni and cheese according to the package directions. If you like mustard on your hot dogs, I recommend mixing up to 1 tablespoon mustard into the cooked macaroni. Air-fry the hot dogs for 8 minutes at 400°F (200°C).
2. Meanwhile, lightly spread the outside of the hot dog buns with butter. Once the hot dogs are done, line up the buns in the air fryer. Add one hot dog per bun, then top with a few tablespoons of macaroni and cheese and a sprinkle of additional cheese to seal in the macaroni. Air-fry for another 8 minutes, until the buns are toasted and the cheese is melted. Top with ketchup and crushed potato chips before serving.

ALTERNATIVE METHOD

To make these in the oven, preheat the oven to 400°F (200°C). Prepare the macaroni and cheese as usual, but bake the hot dogs on a rimmed baking sheet for 10 to 12 minutes (or cook them using your preferred method). Line up the buttered hot dog buns in a casserole dish. Then follow the rest of step 2 and return to the oven instead of the air fryer to finish cooking.

THE PERFECT EGG SANDWICH

When it comes to breakfast sandwiches, I believe more is more—if the filling falls out when you bite into it, you're onto a winner. The possibilities with breakfast sandwiches are endless, and the table and tips below are intended to inspire you—try some of my favorite combinations or use it as a matrix to create your own masterpiece.

SANDWICH	BREAD	SPREAD	EGG STYLE	MEAT	CHEESE	VEGGIES	SEASONING
MORNING PASTRAMI	English muffin	Creamy Dijon mustard	Scrambled	Pastrami	Swiss	Avocado	Everything bagel seasoning
FARMER WRAP	Flour tortilla	Chipotle mayonnaise	Over easy, hard yolk	Bacon	Sharp cheddar	Hash browns	Salt + pepper
BREAKFAST PIZZA TOAST	Sourdough	Pizza sauce	Soft-/medium-boiled	Chopped ham	Mozzarella	Arugula or spinach	Garlic powder
BIG FRENCH TOASTY	French bread	Maple syrup	French toast	Breakfast sausage	Mild or medium cheddar	None	Brown sugar in egg mix
THE CLASSIC VEGGIE, ELEVATED	Multigrain toast	Mayonnaise	Over easy, medium	None	Havarti	Roasted peppers and zucchini	Salt + pepper
THE BLUENOSE	Hamburger bun	Butter	Over easy, soft	Fried bologna	Processed (aka American) cheese	Tomato	Salt + pepper
MORNING STEAK SUB	Sub roll	Hot sauce	Omelet	Steak	Provolone	Sautéed onions + mushrooms	Steak seasoning

HOT TIPS FOR A GREAT BREAKFAST SANDWICH:

1. Pan-toast the bread in a bit of melted butter. Press the slices down to get that salty crisp.
2. Crisp up the toppings. Pan-fry those turkey slices, sauté the onions, melt the cheese—every element gets some love!
3. Season your veggies—salt and pepper will do.
4. Sauce it, but not too much. Eggs are slippery, and it's just annoying to eat a sandwich that's falling apart, if you ask me.

TOFU SCRAMBLE WRAPS

MAKES 5 WRAPS

- 1 tablespoon neutral oil
- 1 (1-pound/454 g) package medium-firm tofu, drained and torn into chunks
- 20 frozen potato tots
- 5 bacon slices (optional)
- 1 tablespoon nutritional yeast (optional)
- 2 teaspoons garlic powder
- 2 teaspoons onion powder
- 1 teaspoon dried parsley
- ½ teaspoon ground turmeric
- ½ teaspoon smoked paprika
- ½ teaspoon salt, plus more to taste
- ⅛ teaspoon pepper, plus more to taste
- ⅓ cup water
- 5 large flour tortillas
- ¼ cup (60 mL) mayonnaise
- 5 cheddar cheese slices
- 1 avocado, peeled, pitted, and chopped (optional)
- 1 tomato, sliced
- 1 cup baby spinach
- Hot sauce, for serving (optional)

Another takeout-inspired tofu recipe? You betcha! But this time we're replacing the scrambled eggs in this loaded breakfast wrap. I love making these ahead, wrapping them in foil, and popping them in the air fryer to reheat. Alex, couldn't you just use eggs? Yup, you could use a lot of things, and you could also just eat the tofu scramble as is. ;)

---

1. Heat the oil in a large skillet over medium heat. Add the tofu and cook, mostly undisturbed but gently flipping every 3 to 5 minutes, until brown, 10 to 15 minutes total, depending on its moisture content. Meanwhile, air-fry the potato tots and bacon (if using).
2. Once the tofu has developed lots of golden bits and most of the water has evaporated, mix together the nutritional yeast (if using), garlic powder, onion powder, parsley, turmeric, smoked paprika, salt, pepper, and water in a small bowl and pour over the tofu. Stir to coat the tofu and cook for a few more minutes, until the water evaporates.
3. Lay out the tortillas and spread with a light coat of mayonnaise. Add a slice of cheese to the center of each, then top with equal amounts of the tofu scramble, potato tots, avocado (if using), tomato, and spinach. Add salt, pepper, and hot sauce, if desired. Wrap up the burritos.
4. Wipe out the pan, then brown the burritos, flipping once, for about 5 minutes total. Serve.

WHY: MEDIUM-FIRM TOFU WILL RESULT IN A MORE EGG-LIKE TEXTURE BUT IS ALSO MORE DELICATE THAN EXTRA-FIRM. AS IT COOKS IT WILL NATURALLY BREAK INTO SMALLER PIECES, BUT IF YOU PRESS IT, YOU'LL END UP WITH MUSH (WHICH TASTES THE SAME BUT DOESN'T LOOK AS NICE).

USE WHAT YOU HAVE

INGREDIENT	TRY THIS INSTEAD:
Tofu	Scrambled eggs (omit turmeric + nutritional yeast)
Potato tots	Leftover roasted potatoes
Bacon	Breakfast sausage, deli ham, second type of cheese
Tomato	Thinly sliced red or orange bell pepper, red onion
Spinach	Arugula or other leafy greens if eating immediately (reheating will make some varieties soggy)

GREEN MONSTER CREPES

MAKES 6 TO 8 CREPES

2 generous handfuls fresh or frozen spinach

¾ cup (185 mL) milk

½ cup (125 mL) water

2 tablespoons lemon juice

2 tablespoons melted butter, plus more for cooking

3 large eggs

1 cup all-purpose flour

1 teaspoon baking powder

½ teaspoon baking soda

¼ teaspoon salt

Optional toppings: Sliced cheese, tomato, ham, sautéed mushrooms and onions, hollandaise sauce

Getting your kids to eat their greens has never been so easy! I use thawed frozen spinach in these green crepes, but you can use fresh if you like, though you may see some speckles. Use their favorite green character to sell these . . . I like to call it "mommy marketing." ;) Add some garlic and onion powder to the crepe mix to make them extra savory, or try a tablespoon or two of honey to make them sweeter instead.

1. Combine all the ingredients (except the toppings!) in a blender or food processor and puree.
2. Heat a nonstick skillet over medium heat, then melt a small pat of butter to grease the pan.
3. For each crepe, pour ⅓ to ½ cup (75 to 125 mL) batter into the pan, depending on the size of the pan, and tilt the pan in circles so the batter spreads thinly toward the edges.
4. Cook undisturbed for 3 to 5 minutes, until the center of the crepe begins to bubble and the edges begin to look cooked, then carefully flip the crepe and cook for another 2 to 3 minutes. Transfer to a plate.
5. Serve while still warm, plain or topped as desired.

OTHER TOPPING IDEAS

SAVORY	SWEET
Chicken + cheddar cheese	Baked apple slices (sliced super thin) + cinnamon sugar
Roasted cherry tomatoes + crumbled feta	Vanilla yogurt (thin smear) + diced peaches

FAVORITE FISH TACOS

MAKES 10 TACOS

10 corn tortillas

2 cups (150 g) shredded cabbage

1 cup (150 g) frozen corn kernels, thawed

¼ cup (60 mL) sour cream or plain Greek yogurt

¼ cup (60 mL) salsa

Juice of ½ lime

¼ cup (30 g) all-purpose flour

1 tablespoon chili powder

1 teaspoon ground cumin

1 teaspoon onion powder

1 teaspoon garlic powder

1 teaspoon salt

Pepper

4 (4-ounce/115 g) white fish fillets, such as cod

2 tablespoons neutral oil

2 avocados, peeled, pitted, and chopped (optional)

½ cup chopped fresh cilantro (optional)

I love finding ways to make serving fresh fish more affordable for my family. These fish tacos are topped with a vibrant fresh cabbage slaw to help fill up the tortillas *and* elevate that beautiful fish. Bonus: Tacos are an especially great family meal since each person can easily customize their own toppings.

---

1. Preheat the oven to 350°F (175°C). Wrap the stack of tortillas in aluminum foil to warm up while you prepare the tacos.
2. Mix together the cabbage, corn, sour cream, salsa, and lime juice in a small bowl; set aside.
3. Mix together the flour, chili powder, cumin, onion powder, garlic powder, salt, and pepper to taste in a shallow bowl. Pat the fish fillets dry with a paper towel, then coat in the flour mixture.
4. Heat the oil in a large nonstick skillet over medium to medium-high heat. Once the oil is hot, gently lower in the fish fillets. Cook undisturbed for 3 to 5 minutes, depending on the thickness of the fillets, then gently flip and cook for another 3 to 5 minutes, or until a meat thermometer inserted reaches at least 145°F (63°C); I prefer my fish cooked to 165°F (74°C). Transfer to a paper towel–lined plate.
5. To assemble the tacos, lightly break up the fish into chunks and distribute evenly between the tortillas, then top with the cabbage slaw, avocado, and cilantro (if using). Serve while still warm.

USE WHAT YOU HAVE

INGREDIENT	TRY THIS INSTEAD:
White fish	Chicken breast (cook to 165°F/74°C)
Corn tortillas	Small flour tortillas
Cabbage	Coleslaw mix, iceberg lettuce
Lime	Lemon
Sour cream	Plain Greek yogurt

ROASTED VEGETABLE BIG BREAD

MAKES 1 LOAF

- 1 head garlic
- Olive oil, for drizzling and brushing
- ¾ teaspoon salt, plus more for garlic
- 2 bell peppers (any color), thinly sliced
- 1 medium yellow onion, thinly sliced
- 1 medium red onion, thinly sliced
- 1 large carrot, peeled and shredded
- 2 cups grape tomatoes
- 1 teaspoon dried basil
- 1 teaspoon dried parsley
- ¼ teaspoon pepper
- 2 tablespoons butter, cut into small cubes
- 1 loaf focaccia or rustic Italian bread, unsliced
- 2 cups (200 g) shredded mozzarella cheese
- 1 cup (100 g) shredded cheddar cheese

If you like anything pizza-adjacent, this recipe is for you. When I was on maternity leave, our budget was very tight so I bought a lot of marked-down (often wrinkly) produce. I came up with this clean-out-the-fridge meal using homemade focaccia (or marked-down bread). The vegetables get irresistibly caramelized and topped with cheese. I've listed which veggies I typically use to get the most bulk while keeping it affordable, but I've included some other choices along with why/why not below. :)

1. Preheat the oven to 400°F (200°C).
2. Cut the top ½ inch (1 cm) off the garlic head and place on a piece of aluminum foil. Drizzle with a bit of oil and sprinkle with salt. Wrap the garlic up in the foil and bake in the oven for 50 minutes. Remove the garlic head from the oven and let cool.
3. Meanwhile, combine the bell peppers, onions, carrot, and tomatoes in a 9 × 13-inch casserole dish and sprinkle with the basil, parsley, salt, and pepper. Dot the butter cubes over the vegetables. Bake until the veggies are caramelized, about 40 minutes, stirring halfway through.
4. In the last 5 minutes of baking, slice the bread in half horizontally and lay out on a rimmed baking sheet. Lightly brush with olive oil and bake for 5 minutes to toast.
5. Squeeze the garlic out of its skins into the vegetable mixture and stir to combine. Spoon onto the toasted bread halves, top with the cheese, and return the dish to the oven for 10 minutes, until the cheese melts and begins to brown. Let cool for a few minutes before cutting into wedges and serving.

WHY: TOASTING THE BREAD WILL HELP IT HOLD UP TO THE MOISTURE FROM THE CARAMELIZED VEGETABLES.

USE WHAT YOU HAVE

GO FOR IT	NEUTRAL	AVOID
Beet, shredded or thinly sliced	Zucchini	Cruciferous veggies like broccoli, cauliflower, or cabbage (will make it bitter)
Corn	Celery, thinly sliced	Cucumber, lettuce (don't cook well)
Large tomatoes, or canned tomatoes (drained)	Mushrooms	Rutabaga (takes too long to cook)
Sweet potato (thinly sliced—adds bulk and sweetness)	Potatoes	Frozen vegetables with the exception of sliced bell peppers (texture will be mushy)

TOASTY CRUDITÉS SANDWICH

MAKES 4 SANDWICHES

QUICK PICKLED ONION

½ cup (125 mL) white vinegar

2 tablespoons sugar

1 teaspoon salt

½ medium red onion, very thinly sliced

SAUCE

½ cup (113 g) mayonnaise

1 tablespoon lemon juice

1 tablespoon yellow mustard

1 tablespoon honey

1 teaspoon garlic powder

¼ teaspoon smoked paprika

¼ teaspoon salt

⅛ teaspoon pepper

SANDWICHES

8 slices soft white bread

½ English cucumber, thinly sliced

Salt and pepper

1 large tomato, thinly sliced

1 bell pepper (any color), thinly sliced

1 carrot, peeled and shredded

1 cup baby spinach

CRONCH! If you love a fresh tomato sandwich, you'll love this one. We use what we have for veggies (except the tomato, you need the tomato), but don't you dare try to put this on whole wheat bread—I'm talking soft, store-bought white, baby—and make it extra saucy! This recipe uses a quick pickled onion, but you can use thinly sliced raw onion if you don't want to make it, or try sliced sweet pickles.

---

1. To make the pickled onion, heat the vinegar, sugar, and salt in a small saucepan. Stir the onion into the vinegar mixture, then turn off the heat and let stand for at least 20 minutes while you prepare the sandwiches. You can also do this step ahead and keep the pickled onion in an airtight container in the refrigerator for up to a week.
2. Meanwhile, mix all the sauce ingredients together in a small bowl.
3. Toast the bread until golden, then spread with the sauce. Layer the cucumber slices on 4 of the toast slices and lightly season with salt and pepper, then add the tomato slices and again lightly season. Top with the bell pepper, carrot, pickled onion, and baby spinach, then close the sandwiches. Cut in half diagonally (the only correct answer) and serve.

NO DELI MEAT SANDWICH TABLE

Deli meat only lasts a day in our house, but sandwiches are forever. We have to get creative between grocery shops, and that's where the no deli meat sandwich table comes in. Not just for lunch, these sandwiches feel special enough for dinner but are quick enough for those busy weeknights when everyone is going in different directions. Of course, feel free to mix and match or just use these ideas as inspiration and sub in whatever you have on hand.

SANDWICH	BREAD	SPREAD	PROTEIN
PEANUT BUTTER & BANANA TACOS	Leftover pancakes	Peanut butter	None
LEFTOVER BUNDLES	Refrigerated crescent rolls	Mayonnaise	Rotisserie chicken
CURRIED EGG SALAD ROLLS	Whole wheat sliced bread	Mayonnaise + drizzle of maple syrup	Boiled eggs
DAD'S CHICKEN PARM SAMMIES	Garlic toast	Pizza sauce	Chicken fingers
PULLED PORK GRILLED CHEESE	Kaiser rolls	Butter	Pulled pork
TACO CRUNCHY WRAPS	Flour tortilla	None	Refried beans
SPAGHETTI & MEATBALL SUBS	Sub rolls	Butter	Leftover spaghetti
TOASTY CRUDITÉS SANDWICH	Toasted white bread	Mayonnaise	None
ROASTED VEGETABLE BIG BREAD	Focaccia	Lightly toss vegetables in oil before roasting	None

CHEESE OR EXTRA FILLING	VEGGIES	SEASONING	ASSEMBLY
Chocolate chips	Sliced banana	Cinnamon	Reheat leftover pancakes in microwave, spread with peanut butter, fill with sliced banana and toppings of choice.
Cheddar	Corn, diced bell pepper, tomato, green onion	Parsley, paprika, salt + pepper	See page 162.
None	Celery, red onion, grated carrot	Curry powder, salt + pepper	Roll bread slices flat with a rolling pin, cut off crusts. Chop and mix together eggs, vegetables, sauces, and seasonings. Fill and roll like sushi.
Mozzarella, Parmesan	None	Parsley for garnish	See page 165.
Mozzarella	Caramelized onion	Pepper	See page 159.
Cheddar	Mashed avocado, chopped tomato	Garlic powder, taco seasoning	Layer ingredients in large flour tortilla. Fold 4 sides in to form a square that overlaps to seal. Heat in pan until the tortilla is crisp.
Mozzarella, Parmesan	None	Salt + pepper	Reheat leftover spaghetti and meatballs, fill sub rolls, top with cheese, broil to melt.
None	Thinly sliced bell pepper, tomato, lettuce	Garlic powder, salt + pepper	See page 179.
Cheddar, mozzarella	Sliced bell pepper, onion, shredded carrot, cherry tomato	Italian seasoning, salt + pepper	See page 176.

CHAPTER SIX

SALADS & VEGGIES

I love a good whole-meal salad. The key? *More is more.* Fresh, crunchy, creamy, salty, sweet, tangy. Hit all those notes and you're in business. Some of these recipes are tried and true to my family, but many were developed when I just grabbed whatever looked good and threw it together. Also included in this section: a few of my go-to quick and easy veggie sides. So start rummaging through your fridge and cupboards and get chopping!

SALAD MATRIX

	GREENS	VEGGIES/FRUIT	PROTEIN	EXTRA TOPPING	DRESSING
BEST TUNA SALAD (PAGE 196)	Romaine lettuce	Coleslaw mix, orange bell pepper, red onion	Canned Tuna	Sunflower seeds	Creamy lemon honey mustard
TACO SALAD	Iceberg lettuce	Tomato, corn	Ground beef	Tortilla chips	Salsa + sour cream
ROASTED ROOT VEGGIE SALAD (PAGE 194)	Baby spinach + arugula	Roasted sweet potato, parsnips	Leftover roast pork or air-fried chickpeas	Sunflower seeds, pumpkin seeds	Maple mustard vinaigrette
COBB SALAD	Chopped romaine lettuce	Corn, tomato, red onion	Boiled egg, diced ham	Croutons	Blue cheese dressing
SWEET & SALTY SPRING MIX SALAD	Spring mix greens	Apple, dried cranberries, sweet onion	Walnuts, pepitas	Hemp hearts	Balsamic vinaigrette
ITALIAN GRINDER SALAD	Green or red leaf lettuce	Tomato, cucumber, red onion	Sliced salami	Croutons	Italian dressing
GREEK SALAD	Romaine lettuce	Tomato, red onion, cucumber	Chicken or none	Olives	Greek yogurt, lemon, olive oil
ASIAN SESAME SALAD	Salad greens	Shredded cabbage, carrot	Shrimp or tofu	Sunflower seeds	Asian sesame dressing

HOW TO MAKE A SALAD DRESSING

Dressings are all about balancing flavors. There are four basic components, and then the rest is kind of up to you. For the ratio, a good place to start is 1 part each fat, acid, and sweetness, plus seasoning. As a tester I recommend starting with about 1 tablespoon each so you aren't wasting a lot of ingredients while you figure out your preference. Personally I like a lot of zing, so my dressings are more like 1 part fat, 2 parts acid, and 1 part sweetness. Then season to your heart's content and dress that salad.

HOT TIP: Reuse an old jar so you can shake everything up and easily store any leftovers in the fridge.

Fat: Neutral oil or olive oil, mayo, Greek yogurt, hummus, or a combination

Acid: Vinegar (any kind), lemon juice, yellow or Dijon mustard, or a combination

Sweetness: Honey, maple syrup, fruit jam, sugar, or a combination

Seasoning: Herbs, spices, salt, pepper

DAD'S CATALINA SALAD

SERVES 4 TO 6

My husband's favorite salad! It's the perfect side dish to accompany BBQ, or have as an easy make-ahead lunch. The base is versatile: you can use iceberg lettuce or cooked pasta, or both. The actual ingredients in this recipe matter less than the way you cut them because the size ratios for each component create the perfect bites.

- 2 cups (250 g) rotini pasta
- 1 large tomato, seeded and diced
- 1 carrot, peeled and shredded
- ½ yellow bell pepper, diced
- ½ English cucumber, quartered lengthwise and sliced crosswise ¼ inch (6 mm) thick
- ¼ medium red onion, diced
- 1 cup (4 ounces/100 g) cubed sharp cheddar cheese (¼ inch/6 mm pieces)
- 2 cups chopped iceberg lettuce

CATALINA DRESSING

- ¼ cup (60 mL) neutral oil
- ¼ cup (60 mL) red wine vinegar
- ¼ cup (50 g) sugar
- 2 tablespoons ketchup
- 1 teaspoon soy sauce
- 1 teaspoon paprika
- ½ teaspoon dried oregano
- ½ teaspoon garlic powder
- ½ teaspoon onion powder
- ¼ teaspoon salt
- ¼ teaspoon pepper

WHY: CUTTING THE CHEESE INTO TINY CUBES INSTEAD OF SHREDDING ENSURES THE DRESSING WON'T PENETRATE AND OVERPOWER ITS FLAVOR.

1. Bring a pot of lightly salted water to a boil and cook the pasta according to the package directions. Drain and set aside to cool.
2. Meanwhile, mix all the dressing ingredients together in a small bowl or jar.
3. Layer the pasta, tomato, carrot, bell pepper, cucumber, onion, and cheese in a large bowl. Pour the dressing over the salad and toss to combine. If you don't like your salad saucy, add the dressing gradually and don't use it all.
4. Refrigerate for at least 20 minutes for the flavors to meld. Mix in the lettuce and serve.

WHY: WAIT TO ADD THE LETTUCE IMMEDIATELY BEFORE SERVING SO IT DOESN'T GET SOGGY.

BTW . . . IF YOU WANT TO USE ONLY PASTA OR ONLY LETTUCE, DOUBLE THE AMOUNT OF THAT INGREDIENT.

GRAMMY'S MANDARIN TURKEY SALAD

SERVES 4 TO 6

This salad is inspired by a simple mandarin orange side salad my mother-in-law makes. Since I can't leave anything alone, I added meat and turned it into a whole meal. It's perfect for a lunch meal-prep but fancy enough for guests—the texture and flavor are bliss. Don't be intimidated by the ingredient list, as most of these are pantry staples you probably already have.

SALAD

¾ cup slivered almonds

1 head green leaf lettuce, cored and chopped

3 green onions, thinly sliced

½ English cucumber, quartered lengthwise and thinly sliced crosswise

1 (10-ounce/284 g) can mandarin oranges in syrup, drained, with ¼ cup (60 mL) syrup reserved for dressing

TURKEY

1 tablespoon neutral oil

1 pound (454 g) ground turkey

2 garlic cloves, minced

1 inch (2.5 cm) piece fresh ginger, peeled and minced

3 or 4 fresh mint leaves, finely chopped (optional)

2 tablespoons brown sugar

2 tablespoons soy sauce

2 tablespoons warm water

1 tablespoon hoisin sauce

¼ teaspoon pepper

¼ teaspoon red pepper flakes (optional)

DRESSING

¼ cup (60 mL) neutral oil

¼ cup (60 mL) white vinegar

2 tablespoons white sugar

¼ teaspoon salt

1. Toast the almonds in a large nonstick skillet over medium heat until they begin to brown, 2 to 3 minutes. Watch them carefully and toss occasionally with a spatula so they don't burn, then transfer to a bowl.
2. Layer the lettuce, green onions, cucumber, and mandarins in a large salad bowl and top with the toasted almonds.
3. To prepare the turkey, heat the oil in the same pan over medium heat. Once the oil is hot, add the turkey and cook until it is no longer pink, breaking it up into bite-size chunks. Traditional ground turkey will take about 8 minutes; the tube style will take longer due to its water content.
4. Combine the garlic, ginger, mint (if using), brown sugar, soy sauce, warm water, hoisin, pepper, and red pepper flakes (if using) in the now-empty almond bowl. (Because less dishes!) Mix until the sugar dissolves, then pour over the turkey. Stir the sauce to coat the turkey and continue cooking for a few minutes, until the liquid is absorbed and the ginger and garlic soften. Let cool for a few minutes, then add to the salad.
5. Meanwhile, prepare the dressing: Mix together the oil, vinegar, reserved mandarin syrup, white sugar, and salt. Pour over the salad and toss to coat. If you don't like your salad saucy, add the dressing gradually; you may not need to use it all. Serve while the turkey is still warm.

continues

USE WHAT YOU HAVE

INGREDIENT	TRY THIS INSTEAD:
Ground turkey	Ground chicken or pork
Green leaf lettuce	1 head or 2 hearts romaine lettuce or 6 cups spring mix
Slivered almonds	Chopped cashews or peanuts

BTW . . . IF YOU WANT TO MEAL-PREP THIS SALAD, KEEP THE TURKEY AND SALAD DRESSING IN SEPARATE CONTAINERS SO YOU CAN REHEAT THE TURKEY BEFORE EATING AND THE SALAD DOESN'T GET SOGGY.

SWEET CHILI SHRIMP SALAD

SERVES 4

CRUNCHY RAMEN CROUTONS (OPTIONAL)

¼ cup (60 g) butter, melted

2 (8-ounce/85 g) packages ramen noodles, seasoning packets reserved for another use

1 tablespoon sesame seeds (optional)

¼ teaspoon salt, plus more to taste

SALAD DRESSING

¼ cup (60 mL) sweet chili sauce

2 tablespoons white vinegar

2 tablespoons mayonnaise

1 tablespoon neutral oil

SALAD

4 cups chopped iceberg lettuce

2 cups coleslaw mix, or finely shredded cabbage and carrot

1 cup chow mein noodles (optional, if not making the croutons)

2 cups (300 g) cooked and peeled shrimp (thawed if frozen), tails removed

3 green onions, sliced

This whole-meal salad hits all the notes and uses lots of super affordable ingredients like crisp cabbage, crunchy ramen croutons, and creamy sweet chili dressing. The special ingredient here is shrimp, and it's so worth it! But if that's not accessible to you, try marinating some cubed extra-firm tofu in a splash of soy sauce, vinegar, and toasted sesame oil instead. Salads are also a great opportunity to clean out your veggie drawer, so feel free to add some extras!

HOT TIP: Don't throw away the ramen seasoning packets! Save them for a future stir-fry or soup.

---

1. If you're making the croutons, preheat an air fryer to 400°F (200°C).
2. Put the melted butter in a medium microwave-safe bowl. Break apart the ramen noodles into ¾-inch (2 cm) pieces and add to the melted butter (some of the ramen will inevitably crumble, so you'll end up with a variety of sizes). Add the sesame seeds (if using) and salt, then toss to coat. Pour the ramen mixture into the air-fryer basket and cook for 3 to 8 minutes, shaking the basket once. **HOT TIP: The cook time varies because some ramen is thin and other brands are thick, so use the lower end for thin ramen and the higher end for thick.** Watch closely as they will go from pale to burnt quickly.
3. Mix together all the salad dressing ingredients in a small bowl.
4. Put the lettuce in a large bowl. Top with the coleslaw mix, ramen croutons or chow mein noodles, shrimp, and green onions. Pour the dressing over, toss to coat, and serve immediately.

BTW . . . IF YOU'RE PLANNING AHEAD, STORE THE RAMEN CROUTONS OR CHOW MEIN NOODLES IN A SEPARATE AIRTIGHT CONTAINER AT ROOM TEMPERATURE UNTIL YOU'RE READY TO DRESS THE SALAD.

MEDITERRANEAN SHRIMP & QUINOA SALAD

SERVES 4

2 teaspoons vegetable bouillon

2 cups (500 mL) water

1 cup quinoa

2 garlic cloves, minced

Juice of ½ lemon

2 tablespoons olive oil

5 ounces (150 g) feta in brine, chopped, plus 2 tablespoons brine

1 teaspoon dried dill

Salt and pepper

¼ red onion, finely chopped

1 cup grape tomatoes, quartered

½ English cucumber, quartered lengthwise and sliced crosswise

1 bell pepper (any color), chopped

2 cups (300 g) cooked and peeled shrimp (thawed if frozen), tails removed

I developed this quinoa salad about a year into my TikTok channel, right after I found out I was being let go from my job. I'll never forget the support I received on that video, so if you've been hanging out in my kitchen long enough to remember this salad, thank you. And if you're new here, thank you too! Feel free to mix up the veggies—these are the ones that feel the most Greek salad–adjacent to me. I call for shrimp as the protein, but canned chickpeas are another great option.

1. Dissolve the bouillon in the water in a small saucepan. Bring to a boil, then add the quinoa and cook for 15 minutes, or according to the package directions. Set aside to cool.
2. Mix together the garlic, lemon juice, oil, feta brine, dill, and salt and pepper to taste in a large bowl. Add the onion, tomatoes, cucumber, bell pepper, quinoa, feta, and shrimp and toss to combine. Serve.

BTW . . . STORE LEFTOVERS IN THE FRIDGE, BUT EAT WITHIN 2 DAYS FOR FOOD SAFETY (BECAUSE OF THE SHRIMP).

ROASTED ROOT VEGGIE SALAD WITH CRUNCHY CROUTONS

SERVES 4

CROUTONS AND SALAD

4 slices stale bread, cut into cubes

2 tablespoons olive oil

½ teaspoon salt

2 to 3 cups (300 to 450 g) chopped roasted root vegetables, such as carrots, sweet potatoes, parsnips

4 cups spring mix salad

⅓ cup dried cranberries

¼ cup sunflower seeds

2 green onions, sliced

2½ ounces (70 g) goat cheese, crumbled

SALAD DRESSING

2 tablespoons balsamic vinegar

1 tablespoon mayonnaise

1 tablespoon olive oil

1 tablespoon honey

1 teaspoon Dijon mustard

½ teaspoon dried summer savory*

½ teaspoon garlic powder

½ teaspoon salt

½ teaspoon pepper

*If you can't find dried summer savory, use a mix of dried ground marjoram, thyme, and oregano.

Give me any excuse to use goat cheese, and this is the perfect one! I love to throw everything in a salad—leftover roasted veggies, stale bread turned into croutons, and homemade salad dressing . . . perfection! Optionally, add some leftover meat or air-fried chickpeas. And check out my salad matrix on page 184 for more ideas on mixing and matching a great salad.

1. Preheat the oven to 400°F (200°C). Line a rimmed baking sheet with parchment paper.
2. Toss the bread cubes with the olive oil and salt on the lined baking sheet, then spread out in a single layer. Bake for about 10 minutes, turning once and watching closely to prevent burning. Spread out the chopped vegetables on a separate rimmed baking sheet and reheat in the oven until warm and crisp, 5 to 10 minutes.
3. In a large bowl, layer the spring mix, root vegetables, cranberries, sunflower seeds, green onions, and goat cheese.
4. Mix together all the dressing ingredients and pour half over the salad. Toss to coat and add more dressing as desired. (I like my salads well dressed, so I usually use it all.) Serve.

USE WHAT YOU HAVE

INGREDIENT	TRY THIS INSTEAD:
Spring mix	Baby spinach, chopped green or red leaf lettuce
Sunflower seeds	Walnut pieces, slivered almonds (replace texture)
Dried cranberries	Chopped apple (replace sweetness)
Goat cheese	Feta cheese, sharp white cheddar, Gorgonzola (replace salt and cheese)

STICKY TOFU LETTUCE WRAPS

MAKES 8 TO 12 LETTUCE WRAPS

LETTUCE WRAPS

1 (1-pound/454 g) package extra-firm tofu, drained

2 tablespoons cornstarch

2 to 4 tablespoons neutral oil

8 to 12 large, pliable lettuce leaves such as Bibb or green leaf

⅓ cup cashews or peanuts, crushed

½ cup chopped fresh cilantro

SAUCE

1 inch (2.5 cm) piece ginger, peeled and minced

3 garlic cloves, minced

2 tablespoons barbecue sauce

2 tablespoons soy sauce

1 tablespoon honey

1 tablespoon white vinegar

1 teaspoon toasted sesame oil

½ teaspoon sriracha, plus more for serving

SLAW

2 carrots, peeled and shredded

¼ medium red onion, thinly sliced

2 tablespoons mayonnaise

½ teaspoon toasted sesame oil

Sriracha

Salt

Back in my vegan era, my husband and I went on a date at Moxies (a cocktail bar and restaurant chain) and I was absolutely floored by how good their tofu lettuce wraps were, which inspired me to re-create them at home. These are super satisfying even sans meat, and since most of the ingredients are standard pantry staples you likely already have, the few ingredients you'll need to buy make this recipe pretty-low cost.

1. Press the tofu to get the water out. **TIP: If you don't have a tofu press, you can wrap the tofu block in a clean dish towel and put a heavy pot on top, pressing down to speed things up.** Cut the tofu into ½-inch (1 cm) cubes and toss in a bowl with the cornstarch.
2. Meanwhile, mix together all the sauce ingredients in a small bowl. Combine all the slaw ingredients in a medium bowl and toss to coat.
3. Heat the oil in a large, heavy-bottomed skillet over medium-high heat. Drop in one piece of tofu to check the oil temperature; if it sizzles, the oil is hot enough. Add the remaining tofu cubes in a single layer, or work in batches if your pan isn't big enough. Cook without disturbing for 2 to 3 minutes, or until the bottom becomes golden brown, then flip and repeat for all sides.
4. Drain off any excess oil from the pan and reduce the heat to medium. Pour in the sauce and cook, stirring frequently, until the sauce thickens and the tofu is coated and sticky, about 5 minutes.
5. To serve, scoop the tofu into lettuce leaves and top with the carrot slaw, cashews or peanuts, cilantro, and sriracha, if you like. If the leaves are large, you can roll them; if they are smaller, fold them and eat like a taco.

SUMMER ROLLS WITH PEANUT SAUCE

MAKES 10 ROLLS

3½ ounces (100 g) vermicelli rice noodles

1 (4.7-ounce/134 g) package rice paper (aka spring roll wrappers)

1 (19-ounce/540 g) can chickpeas, rinsed and drained

1 carrot, peeled and thinly sliced

1 cucumber, thinly sliced

1 avocado, peeled, pitted, and thinly sliced

1 bell pepper (any color), thinly sliced

1 cup baby spinach, chopped

1 cup chopped fresh cilantro

PEANUT SAUCE

½ cup peanut butter

¼ cup warm water

2 tablespoons soy sauce

2 tablespoons apple cider vinegar

1 teaspoon honey

1 teaspoon sriracha (optional)

½ teaspoon toasted sesame oil, plus more to taste

½ teaspoon garlic powder

Listen, these summer rolls are a labor of love, but they are *worth it*. So, when I make them, I'm making a lot. They're perfect to take to a gathering—an affordable but impressive dish everyone always enjoys. Use all or only some of the fillings or try some ideas of your own.

1. Cook the rice noodles according to the package directions, drain, and set aside.
2. Combine all the sauce ingredients in a small bowl and mix until the peanut butter dissolves and no clumps remain. Set aside. **HOT TIP: Microwave the peanut butter for 10 seconds to help it dissolve better.**
3. In a large bowl of warm water, soak one rice paper wrapper until just softened, 30 to 60 seconds, then lay flat on a clean dish towel.
4. Lay out some rice noodles, chickpeas, carrot, cucumber, avocado, bell pepper, spinach, and cilantro in the center of the rice paper. You want the filling to be about 2 inches (4 cm) in diameter, with about one-third rice noodles. Fold the ends of the rice paper over the filling, then fold one side over and wrap tightly but gently to avoid ripping the wrapper. Repeat with the remaining rice paper wrappers until you run out of filling. Serve with the peanut sauce for dipping.

BTW . . . YOU CAN STORE LEFTOVER SUMMER ROLLS IN AN AIRTIGHT CONTAINER IN THE REFRIGERATOR FOR UP TO 2 DAYS. AFTER THAT THEY WILL STILL BE EDIBLE FOR ANOTHER 2 DAYS, BUT THE RICE PAPER WILL START TO DRY OUT. YOU CAN ALSO PAN-FRY LEFTOVER SPRING ROLLS IN A LITTLE OIL FOR A CRISPY VERSION.

continues

USE WHAT YOU HAVE

INGREDIENT	TRY THIS INSTEAD:
Vermicelli rice noodles	Other rice noodles, more spinach, or Bibb lettuce (softer lettuces hold up to moisture)
Vegetables	Finely shredded cabbage, Bibb lettuce, sliced snap peas (avoid bulky vegetables like broccoli and cauliflower, which can tear the rice paper when rolling)
Chickpeas	Cooked shrimp (cold), imitation crab, sliced tofu

FAVORITE ROASTED BROCCOLI

2 TO 4 SIDE SERVINGS

1 head broccoli, cut into florets
1 tablespoon olive oil
2 tablespoons nutritional yeast
½ teaspoon salt

BTW . . . THIS RECIPE IS ALL ABOUT THE BROCCOLI FLORETS, BUT YOU CAN SAVE THE THICK PART OF THE STEM FOR ANOTHER RECIPE, SUCH AS MY PANEER & VEGETABLE KORMA (PAGE 120).

If you're looking to eat a whole head of broccoli like chips, this is the recipe for you. You can also do this with kale, cauliflower, or frozen fine or thin green beans and they are equally great (the roasting time will vary), but frozen broccoli doesn't get as crisp, so save that for my cheese sauce recipe (page 206) instead. If you're making a half recipe, you can do it in the air fryer, but once you try them, you won't want to halve the recipe!

1. Preheat the oven to 400°F (200°C). Line a rimmed baking sheet with parchment paper.
2. Toss the broccoli florets in the oil in a large bowl, then sprinkle on the nutritional yeast and salt and stir to coat. Spread out in an even layer on the lined baking sheet and roast for 15 to 20 minutes, flipping the florets halfway through. I really like a bit of crispy char on my broccoli, but take it out when it's done to your preference. Serve.

CHEESE SAUCE MAKES EVERYTHING BETTER

MAKES ABOUT 1½ CUPS SAUCE

2 tablespoons butter

2 tablespoons all-purpose flour

1 cup (250 mL) milk, or more as needed

2 ounces (50 g) sharp cheddar cheese, shredded (about ½ cup)

Salt and pepper

Like the name says, cheese sauce makes everything better! My daughter requests this for broccoli or cauliflower all the time (it's a great way to elevate those frozen veggies!). I figured out that if you use too much cheese, the sauce tends to break (separate into grainy cheese with oily liquid), so add it slowly—it's cheaper that way anyway!

1. Melt the butter in a small saucepan over medium heat. Stir in the flour and cook for 1 minute, then whisk in the milk until there are no flour lumps. Keep whisking gently until the sauce begins to thicken. Sprinkle in the cheese and mix until fully incorporated. Season with salt and pepper to taste and serve over steamed vegetables of choice.

TIP. . . For a smooth sauce, shred the cheese yourself—preshredded cheese has a coating that doesn't melt as well.

SWEET & SALTY CARAMELIZED CARROTS

MAKES 2 TO 4 SIDE SERVINGS

2 cups baby carrots or carrot sticks cut from large carrots

½ cup (125 mL) water

2 tablespoons butter

¼ cup brown sugar

½ teaspoon salt

I always make this recipe when I have dried-up baby carrots left over since I don't like wasting food. One word of caution: Baby carrots are rinsed in a chlorine mixture that is supposed to be washed off before bagging. I have made these with wet baby carrots and could definitely taste it—so rinse them first. You can also cut your own fresh carrots into sticks.

---

1. Combine the carrots and water in a nonstick skillet and steam over medium heat until the water cooks off, about 5 minutes. Add the butter and brown sugar, stirring to coat while they melt, and cook until the sauce thickens and the carrots are caramelized, 10 to 15 minutes (this takes longer for baby carrots as they tend to release more moisture). The carrots are done when you can pierce them easily with a fork but they still have some firmness to them. Season with the salt and serve.

CHAPTER SEVEN

SNACKS & DIPS

If you want to win Mom of the Year while cleaning out your fridge and pantry, snack trays are my favorite way to use up things nobody is reaching for; everyone loves a little of this and that! You're probably thinking of the half bag of baby carrots in your veggie drawer, but I'm also talking about those last few slices of bread that aren't enough to feed everyone—quarter a couple of PB&Js, and suddenly two sandwiches multiply into eight.

MIX & MATCH SNACKS

Now anything goes, but for me there is some strategy involved in making a super-balanced snack-supper you can serve day after day sans mom-guilt. This table is full of ideas you can mix and match for your next everything platter. But don't let it limit you!

FRUITS + VEGGIES (½ TRAY)	PROTEIN (¼ TRAY)	GRAINS & STARCHES (¼ TRAY)
Crudités—try rutabaga sticks!	Rotisserie chicken	Potato tots/French fries
Whole Snack Smoothie (page 233)	Boiled eggs	Mini pancakes
Crispy air-fried veggies	Energy Pop Bites (page 226)	Naan mini-pizzas
Thawed frozen mango chunks	Rolled deli meat	Bagel rounds (cut sideways, toasted or not)
Cream Cheese Stuffed Bell Peppers (page 234)	Nuts (not for kids under 4)	Popcorn (not for kids under 4)
Cut fresh fruit	Strawberry Cheesecake Fruit Dip (page 227)	Quartered sandwiches/wraps
Pickles + olives	Hummus	Crackers, tortilla chips
Veggie Cornbread Galettes (page 215)	Crispy Air Fryer Tofu Bites (page 214)	Mini muffins, Sneaky Apple-Lentil Muffins (page 220)
Dried fruit	Cheese	Stuffed mini pita pockets
Ants on a log	Lentil Nuggets with Yogurt Sauce (page 216)	Fun cereal, loose or in Mixed-Up Cereal Marshmallow Squares (page 229)

SALMON SUSHI ROLLS

MAKES 10 ROLLS

1½ cups (300 g) sticky brown rice

1¾ cups (435 mL) water

1 tablespoon white vinegar, plus more for sealing rolls

1 tablespoon sugar

¼ teaspoon salt, plus more for salmon

1 pound (454 g) salmon fillet

¼ cup (60 mL) mayonnaise

½ teaspoon sriracha

½ teaspoon toasted sesame oil

10 sushi nori (seaweed sheets)

1 large carrot, peeled and thinly sliced or cut into ribbons with a peeler

½ English cucumber, halved lengthwise and thinly sliced crosswise

2 avocados, peeled, pitted, and sliced

Sesame seeds, for topping (optional)

Soy sauce, for dipping

You guys, sushi is dang expensive, and it's not nearly as hard to prepare yourself as you'd think. When I worked at the grocery store, I got a quick rundown from our in-house sushi guy, and although I'm not brave enough to use raw fish—you do you! (We use what we have in terms of comfort level too.) You can also make this as a sushi bowl instead of wrapping. Cut the seaweed wraps into little strips—you'll only need a few sheets.

---

1. Add the rice, water, vinegar, sugar, and salt to an electric pressure cooker. Pressure cook on high for 20 minutes, then let it release naturally. (Alternatively, you can cook the rice on the stovetop according to the package directions.) **HOT TIP: I recommend *not* rinsing the rice as we need that starch for it to stick together.**

2. Meanwhile, lightly salt the salmon and air-fry or bake it at 350°F (175°C) until the internal temperature reaches at least 145°F (63°C), 12 to 15 minutes. Let cool for a few minutes, then flake the fish into a bowl with a fork. Mix in the mayonnaise, sriracha, and sesame oil.

3. Prepare the sushi rolls while the rice is still warm but not too hot to handle. Lay out a sheet of seaweed on a clean folded dish towel (or a sushi mat if you have one) and scoop ⅓ cup rice into the center. Use the back of the measuring cup to spread the rice out, leaving an inch or so on two sides, like a big rice stripe. Spread about ¼ cup of the salmon mixture along the center of the rice, then layer on some carrot, cucumber, and avocado. Sprinkle with sesame seeds, if using.

4. Pour a little vinegar into a small dish, then brush a bit along the seaweed borders to wet them. Roll the sushi up and press gently to glue the edges together, adding more vinegar to the seam if needed. In the name of skipping more steps, I dip and munch these rolls as they are, but you can cut them. Dip a very sharp knife in vinegar every few slices to avoid rice gumming up the knife. Repeat to form the remaining rolls. Serve with soy sauce for dipping.

continues →

BTW . . . MOST SHORT-GRAIN RICE IS STICKIER THAN LONG-GRAIN, BUT I LIKE TO CHOOSE ONE THAT SPECIFICALLY SAYS IT'S STICKY. SUSHI RICE OF COURSE IS IDEAL, BUT LESS ACCESSIBLE AND REQUIRES RINSING OR IT'LL BE GLUGGY, WHICH IS AN EXTRA STEP.

USE WHAT YOU HAVE

OTHER FILLINGS TO TRY:
Imitation crab
Green onion
Leftover sweet potato fries
Marinated mushroom slices
Cooked shrimp

CRISPY AIR FRYER TOFU BITES

SERVES 2 TO 4 AS A SNACK

- 1 (1-pound/454 g) package extra-firm tofu, drained
- 1 tablespoon neutral oil
- 1 tablespoons soy sauce
- 1 tablespoon cornstarch
- 2 teaspoons garlic powder
- 2 teaspoon onion powder
- 2 teaspoons paprika
- Ketchup, for dipping

My kids will eat tofu plain out of the package, which is a bit bland for me. I prefer it doused in seasoning and air-fried until the outside is crisp and the inside is pillowy (or chewy depending on my mood that day). These are an easy protein to throw together on a snacky supper night—dip in your favorite sauce or ketchup.

1. Press the water out of the tofu. You can use a tofu press or wrap the block in a clean dish towel and place something heavy on it for about 20 minutes. Getting the water out is important—nobody wants to eat a wet sponge.
2. Slice the tofu block in half lengthwise, then into ½-inch (1 cm) sticks and place in a bowl. Pour over the oil, soy sauce, cornstarch, garlic powder, onion powder, and paprika. Very gently stir to coat. Some of them will inevitably break, but do your best.
3. Air-fry at 400°F (200°C) in a single layer for 10 to 15 minutes, tossing halfway through. **HOT TIP: Don't crowd the air fryer, or the tofu won't get crispy.** The cook time will depend how well you pressed the water out, the tofu will be drying as it cooks. The outside should be crispy but the inside will still be soft. Let cool slightly, then serve with ketchup or your favorite dipping sauce.

VEGGIE CORNBREAD GALETTES (PANCAKES)

MAKES 8 TO 10 GALETTES

I'm a savory girl all day every day, so I rarely go for traditional muffins, but it's nice to have some grab-and-go options, so I created these cheesy, veggie-filled, corn muffin–inspired galettes (French for pancakes).

Each time I tried to make these into mini muffins, they would stick to the muffin tin no matter how well I greased it, so I decided to pan-fry them instead. Store leftovers in an airtight container in the refrigerator for up to 5 days.

GALETTES

- 1 small carrot, peeled and shredded
- ½ medium zucchini, shredded
- ½ cup (50 g) shredded sharp cheddar cheese
- ½ cup (125 g) cottage cheese
- 2 large eggs
- ½ cup (60 g) yellow cornmeal
- ½ cup (60 g) all-purpose flour
- 1 teaspoon onion powder
- 1 teaspoon garlic powder
- 1 teaspoon paprika
- 1 teaspoon baking powder
- ½ teaspoon salt
- ¼ teaspoon pepper

FOR PAN-FRYING

- 2 to 4 tablespoons neutral oil

1. Mix together all the galette ingredients in a large bowl and let sit for 5 minutes for the cornmeal to absorb the liquid.
2. Meanwhile, heat a tablespoon or so of oil in a large nonstick skillet over medium heat. Working in batches, scoop ¼ cup batter per galette into the pan and flatten to ½ inch (1 cm) thick with the back of the scoop. **QUICK TIP: Using a cookie or ice cream scoop saves time and mess.** Cook for 3 to 5 minutes per side, until the galettes are browned and cooked through. Transfer to a cooling rack or a paper towel–lined plate. Add more oil as needed for subsequent batches. Serve warm.

WHY: IF YOU PUT THE GALETTES DIRECTLY ON A PLATE, THE CONDENSATION FROM THE WARM FOOD WILL MAKE THEM SOGGY.

USE WHAT YOU HAVE

INGREDIENT	TRY THIS INSTEAD:
Carrot and zucchini	Diced bell pepper and minced onion
½ cup cottage cheese	More shredded cheese (any kind)
Cornmeal	Additional all-purpose flour

LENTIL NUGGETS WITH YOGURT SAUCE

MAKES 10 TO 12 NUGGETS

FRITTERS

1 cup (200 g) red lentils

2 large eggs

1 tablespoon nutritional yeast (optional)

2 teaspoons garlic powder

2 teaspoons onion powder

1 teaspoon dried oregano

1 teaspoon smoked paprika

½ teaspoon salt

¼ teaspoon pepper

½ cup panko breadcrumbs

2 to 4 tablespoons neutral oil

YOGURT SAUCE

½ cup (125 mL) plain Greek yogurt

2 teaspoons lemon juice

2 teaspoons dried dill

1 teaspoon garlic powder

¼ teaspoon salt

WHY: THIS WILL HELP THE NUGGETS HOLD TOGETHER BETTER.

This is the recipe that made me known as the Lentil Lady on TikTok. It's only three ingredients plus spices so it's nearly free. My lentil nuggets are a nod to Indian fritters but are definitely not traditional. You can switch up the seasoning and dipping sauce based on what you have and the flavors you prefer.

1. Soak the lentils in a bowl of room-temperature water overnight. **HOT TIP: If you are short on time, pour boiling water over the bowl of lentils, then cover it with a plate to keep the heat in and soak for 1 hour.** Drain.
2. Combine the lentils, eggs, nutritional yeast (if using), garlic powder, onion powder, oregano, smoked paprika, salt, and pepper in a food processor and roughly puree. Mix in the breadcrumbs and let sit for 5 minutes to absorb.
3. Meanwhile, mix together all the yogurt sauce ingredients in a bowl and set aside.
4. Heat the oil in a large skillet over medium-high heat. Drop in a small amount of the lentil mixture and if it sizzles, the oil is hot enough. Working in batches, drop in spoonfuls (2 to 3 tablespoons each) of the lentil mixture and lightly flatten with the back of the spoon, leaving space in between. Cook undisturbed until the bottoms brown, 3 to 5 minutes, then flip and cook for another 3 to 5 minutes, until the other side browns and the fritters are firm.
5. Transfer the fritters to a paper towel–lined plate to drain. Allow the oil to get hot again before starting the next batch. Serve with the yogurt sauce.

WHY: FRYING IN OIL THAT ISN'T HOT ENOUGH CAUSES THE FOOD TO ABSORB MORE OIL AND BECOME GREASY.

PIZZA BEAN DIP

SERVES 4 AS A MEAL OR 8 AS AN APPETIZER

- 2 (19-ounce/540 g) cans white kidney beans (cannellini), rinsed and drained
- 1 (16- to 24-ounce/454 to 600 g) jar marinara sauce (whichever you have on hand)
- 1 teaspoon chicken bouillon
- 1 teaspoon garlic powder
- 1 teaspoon onion powder
- 1 teaspoon dried basil
- ¼ teaspoon pepper
- ½ cup (125 mL) water
- 1 baguette or other artisan bread, thinly sliced
- Olive oil, for drizzling
- 1 garlic clove, peeled and halved
- 2 cups (200 g) shredded mozzarella cheese
- ½ cup (50 g) grated Parmesan cheese
- Chopped fresh parsley, for garnish

If there's tomato sauce and cheese in it, I'm gonna call it pizza every time. And if I call it pizza, my kids are automatically on board. Between us, these pizza beans are just beans on toast with a twist . . . Shhh! ;) White kidney beans are soft and absorb the tomato flavor well, but you can also try white navy beans since that's what's typically used in baked beans. If eating on toast, I recommend using a knife and fork as it can get messy.

1. Preheat the oven to 400°F (200°C).
2. Add the beans, marinara sauce, bouillon, garlic powder, onion powder, basil, and pepper to a large, broiler-safe skillet. Pour the water into the marinara jar and shake to catch the remaining sauce, then pour into the pan. Cook the beans over medium heat, stirring occasionally, until the sauce comes to a simmer, then reduce to medium-low, cover, and cook for 20 minutes.
3. Meanwhile, lay the baguette slices in a single layer on a rimmed baking sheet. Lightly drizzle with olive oil. Toast in the oven for 5 minutes, then rub with the cut sides of the garlic clove.
4. Turn the oven to broil, top the bean mixture with the cheeses, and broil for 3 to 5 minutes, until the cheese bubbles and begins to brown. Let sit for 5 minutes, then garnish with parsley. To serve, scoop up the bean mixture with the toast rounds.

WHY: THE ROUGH TEXTURE OF THE TOAST WILL MICRO-GRATE THE GARLIC, GIVING THE BAGUETTE A NICE FLAVOR.

BTW . . . MAKE THESE INTO PERSONAL PIZZA DIPS BY DIVIDING INTO BROILER-SAFE RAMEKINS BEFORE BAKING.

SNEAKY APPLE-LENTIL MUFFINS

MAKES 24 MINI MUFFINS

½ cup (100 g) red lentils

2 large apples, cored and roughly chopped

2 large eggs

2 tablespoons neutral oil

1 teaspoon vanilla

1½ cups (180 g) all-purpose flour

½ cup (105 g) brown sugar

1 teaspoon ground cinnamon, plus more for topping (optional)

1 teaspoon baking soda

½ teaspoon salt

GLAZE (OPTIONAL)

½ cup (55 g) confectioners' sugar

2 tablespoons milk

When I find a recipe that makes it easy to hide nutrient powerhouse ingredients my kids may not otherwise be willing to eat—you know I'll be making it on repeat! Adding lentils to muffins is one of my most viral mom hacks. When you soak and then blend red lentils, they become completely unrecognizable in these apple-flavored muffins.

1. Soak the lentils in a bowl of room-temperature water overnight. **HOT TIP: If you are short on time, pour boiling water over the bowl of lentils, then cover it with a plate to keep the heat in and soak for 1 hour.** Drain.
2. Preheat the oven to 425°F (220°C). Spray a mini muffin tin with nonstick cooking spray.
3. Pulse the apples in a food processor. If you like, set aside ¼ cup of the finely chopped apples for topping. Put the remaining apples in a large bowl.
4. Put the lentils and eggs in the food processor and puree, then transfer to the bowl with the apples. Mix in the oil and vanilla. Add the flour, brown sugar, cinnamon, baking soda, and salt and stir to combine.
5. Spoon the batter into the prepared muffin tin—I like to use a small cookie scoop. If topping with the reserved chopped apple and additional cinnamon, sprinkle them on now. Bake for 5 minutes, then reduce the oven temperature to 375°F (190°C) and bake for another 5 minutes, or until a toothpick inserted comes out clean. Remove the muffins from the oven and let cool for 5 minutes before removing them from the muffin tin.
6. If you like, mix together the confectioners' sugar and milk in a bowl to make a glaze. Drizzle lightly over the muffins, then serve.

USE WHAT YOU HAVE

INGREDIENT	TRY THIS INSTEAD:
2 large eggs	2 tablespoons ground flax + 6 tablespoons water; mix and let set for 5 minutes to thicken
½ cup brown sugar	½ cup white sugar + 1 to 2 teaspoons molasses
1 teaspoon baking soda	1½ teaspoons baking powder

PEANUT BUTTER–BANANA OAT BARS

MAKES 1 LOAF

3 overripe bananas

¾ cup (200 g) peanut butter

⅓ cup (75 mL) maple syrup

2 teaspoons vanilla extract

3 cups (250 g) quick rolled oats

3 tablespoons ground flax, (optional)

1½ teaspoons ground cinnamon

¼ teaspoon salt

⅔ cup chocolate chips

These breakfast bars were my go-to postpartum breakfast because they are packed with protein and fiber, and are so easy to make I could usually manage it one handed (IYKYK). If you are meal-prepping, these can be stored in an airtight container for a few days. I use regular-shmegular peanut butter, but any nut butter works.

1. Preheat the oven to 375°F (190°C). Line a loaf pan with parchment paper.
2. Mash together the bananas, peanut butter, maple syrup, and vanilla in a medium bowl. Stir in the oats, flax (if using), cinnamon, salt, and most of the chocolate chips, reserving about 2 tablespoons for the top. Pour the mixture into the lined loaf pan and press down to flatten. Sprinkle the reserved chocolate chips across the top.
3. Bake for 40 to 50 minutes, or until the loaf is firm and the edges are golden. Let cool for at least 10 minutes, then remove from the pan by pulling up the parchment paper. Slice into bars and serve.

USE WHAT YOU HAVE

INGREDIENT	TRY THIS INSTEAD:
Chocolate chips	Frozen blueberries (cook time may increase due to moisture) or double the maple syrup
Peanut butter	Almond butter

QUICK OAT GRANOLA

6 TO 8 SERVINGS

4 cups (340 g) quick oats
2 tablespoons ground flax
2 teaspoons ground cinnamon
½ teaspoon salt
½ cup olive oil
½ cup maple syrup
1½ cups salad topper mix
¼ cup unsweetened coconut flakes (optional)
½ cup chocolate chips

Every time I buy the giant bag of salad topper mix it ends up sitting in the back of my cupboard for months . . . until I started using it in granola. Now, instead of buying a bunch of nuts, seeds, and dried fruit individually (which really add up!), I buy one of these bags and it makes the best granola mix-in. This recipe uses quick oats because we use what we have, and that's what I always have!

1. Preheat the oven to 325°F (160°C). Line a rimmed baking sheet with parchment paper.
2. Combine the oats, flax, cinnamon, salt, olive oil, and maple syrup in a bowl, stirring to coat evenly.
3. Spread the oat mixture evenly on the lined baking sheet, pressing everything down with a spatula.
4. Bake for 30 minutes, then gently flip the granola and bake for another 10 to 15 minutes. Keep a close eye after flipping—you want the oats to get toasty golden, but the path from brown to burnt is short. Your exact cook time will depend on how thin you spread the oats.
5. Allow the granola to cool completely, then mix in the salad topper, coconut (if using), and chocolate chips. Store in an airtight container for up to a week or in the freezer for future use.

WHY: SQUISHING THE OATS TOGETHER IS WHAT MAKES THOSE DELICIOUS GRANOLA CLUSTERS.

WHY: DISTURBING THE GRANOLA WHILE IT'S STILL HOT WILL BREAK UP THE CLUSTERS.

USE WHAT YOU HAVE

INGREDIENT	TRY THIS INSTEAD:
Salad topper blend	Any mix of chopped nuts, seeds, and dried fruit
Olive oil	Any neutral vegetable oil, but it won't have that savory depth
Maple syrup	¼ cup honey mixed with 2 tablespoons hot water to thin it out

ENERGY POP BITES

MAKES 15 TO 20 BALLS

- 1 cup (85 g) quick oats
- 2 tablespoons ground flax
- 2 tablespoons chia seeds
- ⅓ cup dried cranberries
- 3 tablespoons mini chocolate chips
- ¼ teaspoon ground cinnamon
- ½ cup (135 g) peanut butter
- 2 tablespoons hot water
- 1 tablespoon honey
- 1 teaspoon vanilla extract

I make these for easy grab-and-go snacks in between grocery shops when the kids have eaten all the packaged snacks. A lot of energy ball recipes are high in sugar, so I set out to see how little I could use before they didn't stick together—I figured out the solution is actually using traditional peanut butter, quick oats, and a bit of hot water.

1. Stir together the oats, flax, chia seeds, cranberries, chocolate chips, and cinnamon in a medium bowl, then add the peanut butter, hot water, honey, and vanilla and mix to combine thoroughly.
2. To make each energy ball, press about 1 tablespoon of the mixture into a ball with clean hands. Compress the mixture so it holds together. **TIP: Do not roll them lightly like a meatball—they will fall apart.** Store in an airtight container in the refrigerator for up to 1 week.

USE WHAT YOU HAVE

INGREDIENT	TRY THIS INSTEAD:
Quick oats	Rolled oats (you'll need more honey to bind)
Peanut butter	Other nut butter (you'll need more honey to bind)
1 tablespoon honey	2 tablespoons maple syrup, reduce hot water
Ground flax, chia seeds	Increase either one to 3 tablespoons (don't double or you'll have a too-much-of-a-good-thing situation)
Dried cranberries	Raisins or any chopped dried fruit
Chocolate chips	Increase honey to make up the sweetness

CINNAMON CRUNCH & STRAWBERRY CHEESECAKE FRUIT DIPS

MAKES 3 CUPS

CINNAMON CRUNCH

1 cup vanilla Greek yogurt

¼ cup (65 g) peanut butter

2 tablespoons maple syrup

¼ teaspoon ground cinnamon

STRAWBERRY CHEESECAKE

1 cup strawberry Greek yogurt

½ cup cream cheese, at room temperature

2 tablespoons maple syrup

FRUIT

Fresh fruit (such as apple slices, strawberries, and kiwi slices), for dipping

I'm all about pairing produce with protein as a healthy snack for myself and my kids. When paired with apple slices, one of these tastes like Cinnamon Toast Crunch cereal—your mind will be blown. And the other tastes like strawberry cheesecake. You'll be eating fruit like never before, trust me.

1. Mix all the ingredients for each dip in a small bowl. Serve with cut-up fruit for dipping.

MIXED-UP CEREAL MARSHMALLOW SQUARES

MAKES 9 LARGE SQUARES

1 (14-ounce/400 g) package mini marshmallows, divided

½ cup (115 g) butter, divided

9 cups mixed cereal (I used 3 cups each Corn Pops, Lucky Charms, and Golden Grahams), divided

3 to 4 chocolate bars, chopped (optional; I like a mix of Mars bars and white chocolate), divided

Cereal is often on multi-deals where I live, so I end up with three half-eaten boxes in my cupboard at any given time. Turns out that's perfect for mixing up with a couple of chopped chocolate bars and suddenly you have every kid's (and adult's) dream dessert.

1. Spray a 9 × 9-inch casserole dish with nonstick cooking spray.
2. Divide all the ingredients in half in separate bowls.
3. Melt half of the marshmallows and half of the butter in a microwave-safe bowl in 30-second increments, 60 to 90 seconds in total, stirring in between. Working quickly, mix in half of the cereal and half of the chocolate until the cereal is fully coated. Transfer to the prepared casserole dish and press down on the mixture to create a tight, even layer. **HOT TIP: Lay plastic wrap over the cereal mixture before pressing down to keep it from sticking to your hands.** Repeat the process with the remaining ingredients, pressing the mixture down on top of the first layer in the casserole dish.
4. Let cool completely, at least an hour. Cut into 9 bars and serve. Store leftovers in an airtight container at room temperature for up to 4 days (after that they are still food safe but will end up hard and stale—I don't make the rules).

WHY: THIS NEEDS TO BE DONE IN TWO BATCHES SINCE IT WON'T ALL FIT IN A BOWL THAT FITS IN THE MICROWAVE, AND YOU NEED TO BE READY TO STIR RIGHT AWAY WHEN THE MARSHMALLOWS ARE MELTED OR THEY WILL NOT COAT THE CEREAL EVENLY.

BTW . . . MINI MARSHMALLOWS WORK BEST SINCE THEY MELT MORE EVENLY AND DON'T RISK SEIZING UP, BUT YOU CAN USE REGULAR MARSHMALLOWS—THEY JUST TAKE LONGER TO MELT, AND YOU'LL WANT TO WORK QUICKLY ONCE THEY DO.

GREEK YOGURT BANANA SPLITS

MAKES 4 BANANA SPLITS

2 cups (500 mL) 2% vanilla Greek yogurt, divided

1 (3.4-ounce/96 g) package vanilla instant pudding mix, divided

1 cup (250 mL) 2% strawberry Greek yogurt

1 tablespoon cocoa powder

1 tablespoon maple syrup

4 bananas

Optional toppings: chocolate sauce, whipped cream, crushed peanuts, sprinkles, maraschino cherries

A couple of times every summer I take my kids out for ice cream for dinner (versus for dessert) and it's absolutely a core memory for everyone. I wanted to make it something we could do more frequently at home, so I set out to make Greek yogurt, which is high in protein, scoopable like ice cream. Turns out the secret is dry pudding mix, and that's how breakfast banana splits were born.

---

1. Beat 1 cup of the vanilla Greek yogurt and 2 tablespoons of the vanilla pudding mix with an electric mixer in a large mixing bowl until peaks form and the yogurt is thick like mousse, about 2 minutes. Transfer to a small freezer-safe container and put in the freezer to set up for 30 to 60 minutes. Repeat with the strawberry Greek yogurt and another 2 tablespoons vanilla instant pudding mix, using a separate container. Repeat again with the remaining 1 cup vanilla Greek yogurt, 2 tablespoons vanilla instant pudding mix, cocoa powder, and maple syrup in a third container.
2. Peel the bananas and slice lengthwise. Place each in an oblong bowl. (Alternatively, you can slice the bananas crosswise and serve in a regular round bowl like a sundae.) Use an ice cream scoop to place one scoop of each flavor of yogurt in a row on each banana. Top with your toppings of choice and serve.

Vitamix

WHOLE SNACK SMOOTHIE

MAKES 2 LARGE OR 4 SMALL SMOOTHIES

- 2 cups ice cubes
- 1 cup (250 mL) orange juice
- ½ cup (125 mL) plain Greek yogurt
- ⅓ cup quick oats
- 1 cup baby spinach
- 1 overripe banana
- ½ cup (75 g) frozen raspberries
- 2 tablespoons peanut butter
- 1 tablespoon chia seeds
- 1 tablespoon ground flax
- 1 tablespoon honey
- 1 teaspoon vanilla extract

My sister-in-law makes her kids a smoothie every morning. She made it at my house one Christmas, and since their cousins like it, my kids do too! I recreated it with measurements, so you can too. It has everything you need in a liquid snack.

1. Blend all the ingredients in a blender until smooth. Serve immediately, as the flax and chia seeds will thicken the smoothie if left to sit. If not serving immediately, shake vigorously before serving.

OTHER COMBINATIONS I LIKE

SWAP THIS:	FOR THIS:
Oats + orange juice	Overripe banana + milk
Raspberries	Blueberries
Plain Greek yogurt + vanilla + honey	Vanilla yogurt

CREAM CHEESE STUFFED BELL PEPPERS, THREE WAYS

MAKES 18 PIECES

9 mini sweet bell peppers, halved lengthwise and seeded

1 cup cream cheese

1 tablespoon balsamic glaze

Sea salt

3 tablespoons pizza sauce

¼ cup shredded cheddar cheese

1 tablespoon honey mustard (equal parts honey and mustard)

1 medium dill pickle, thinly sliced

1 tablespoon everything bagel seasoning

If I'm making a charcuterie board, I'm absolutely adding these stuffed mini peppers every time—They're crunchy, fresh, savory, and super quick to make. I've included three varieties, but my favorite is the balsamic glaze, so definitely don't skip that one!

1. Spread each pepper half with ½ to 1 tablespoon cream cheese, depending on the size of the pepper. You want a generous amount for flavor but not so thick as to overpower.
2. For 6 of the bell pepper halves, drizzle balsamic glaze over the cream cheese and sprinkle with sea salt. For another 6, spread with pizza sauce and sprinkle with cheddar cheese. Top the remaining 6 with honey mustard, dill pickle, and everything bagel seasoning. Serve immediately.

ACKNOWLEDGMENTS

This book would not be possible without the dedication of my support system. Writing a cookbook has been a dream of mine for years, and I have so many people to thank.

To my family and friends: My husband Andrew—who trusts and supports me without question. Thanks for letting me take risks and holding down the fort on a moment's notice. Your stability allows me to chase my dreams, and I'm forever grateful you chose me to do life with. To my kids, my reason and my world, for being the three best little hecklers and for accepting that you'll probably have to try a different meal every night until basically forever. Thanks for thinking my job is really cool and rolling with everything that comes with. To my dad, who told me "you can be anything you want, but you need to be the best at it," instilling commitment, drive, and hard work into me. And my mom, for always letting me cook but never making me do the dishes; for teaching me about money, value, and how to find a deal; but most importantly, for speaking confidence into me as a child, which became my internal voice as an adult.

To my followers, my people . . . you really get me. You pump me up, teach me things, share your stories, laugh at my jokes, and even through the screen I can feel it—you have my back. I can't thank you enough for showing up daily to spend a few precious minutes hanging out in my kitchen with me. Your continued support means the world to me—it's the reason I've been able to turn my passion into a career, and without you this book wouldn't exist.

Special thanks to my team, who worked tirelessly on this cookbook: My photographer, food stylist, and friend, Jessica Emin, and her assistant, Katie Tower, for spending three straight weeks in my kitchen with me making my not-always-aesthetic food look mouth-watering. My Countryman Press team: Ann Treistman, editorial director, for managing this project and my emotions all in one. Devorah Backman, for believing in my content and skills enough to recommend me for this book. Allison Chi, for bringing my design vision to life. And to my book agent, Alison Fargis, for her guidance and support. My recipe testers: Penny Layman, Julie Scott, Kevin Lemieux, Sophia Butt, Holly Greca, and Daniel Burke. Finally, thanks to my friend Jennifer Joyce for taking countless meals off my hands and giving me honest feedback during the recipe development phase.

INDEX

Note: Page references in *italics* indicate photographs.

C

D

E

F

G

Q

R

S

T

U

V

W

Y

Z